EXPONENTIAL INFLUENCE®

DESIGNING DIGITAL HABITS

THAT ENGAGE

DISTRACTED CUSTOMERS

The Exponential Influence®
Book Series

Exponential Influence is a series of fast-reading books published by Exponential Edge Inc. that enable executives to rapidly learn about leading-edge neuroscience, motivation, marketing, leadership, and technology strategies from the Silicon Valley and beyond. Filled with practical case studies and ideas, the series helps you to apply the latest techniques to increase your business and personal success.

Books in the series include:

- Designing Digital Habits That Engage Distracted Customers

- Energize Your Customer Attraction Zone

Future books planned in the series include:

- Best Practices for the Digital Customer Journey

- Designing Digital Habits for Health

- Strategic Alliances and Channel Partnerships

- Expanding Personal Influence

- Engaging Distracted Employees

Praise for *Exponential Influence* and Adrian C. Ott

"One of Silicon Valley's most respected (if not the most respected) strategists."
Consulting Magazine

"Exponential Influence is full of 10X ways the C-Suite and marketers can triumph over digital distractions!"

Jeffrey Hayzlett
Primetime TV and Radio Host
Author, Speaker and sometime-cowboy

"Breakthrough thinking!! Loyalty is the principle of brand equity and is usually based in part on habitual behavior. Adrian applies this logic to digital behavior and show how digital habits form and how they can be influenced. To make your digital programs succeed you need to understand digital habits and how they can be influenced. This book takes you there. A must read."

David Aaker
Vice Chairman, Prophet
Professor Emeritus and Author, U.C. Berkeley

"Your customers have acquired something new: digital habits. In her new book, *Exponential Influence—Digital Habits*, Adrian Ott reveals how digital habits are driving customer behavior, and then she shows you the steps and resources you need to become more habit forming than your competitors."

Jim Blasingame
Host of The Small Business Advocate Show
Author, *The Age of the Customer: Prepare for the Moment of Relevance*

ii

"The *Exponential Influence* series is a must read for today's Chief Marketing Officers, strategy and digital executives who seek innovative ideas to get to the top of their career. Digital technologies have dramatically altered how companies market to, listen to, interact with and serve customers. The Exponential Influence books help executives to remain relevant in leading their organization with cutting-edge business, digital marketing, and technology strategies."

Kathryn Ullrich
Principal, Heidrick & Struggles
Author, *Getting to the Top:*
Strategies for Career Success

"Adrian is masterful at cutting through jargon with insightful approaches that shed light on the new way executives must think to remain relevant in this age of rapid innovation. Ground-breaking - *Exponential Influence* is a must-read that will provoke you to get up and change the way you do business in the digital age."

Ping Hao
Co-President & Board Member
Harvard Business School Association
Northern California

"Adrian has always had a unique ability to see how several different trends are coming together to form something completely new. But more important, she's been able to help me see how to take advantage of the opportunities presented by the convergence of trends."

Janice Chaffin
President (retired)
Consumer Business
Symantec

"Adrian Ott and her team worked with us as a catalyst to redirect our business strategy based on disruptive technology changes affecting our marketplace. The Exponential Edge team provided an external voice of reason-validating and shaping our approach through market research, opportunity sizing, trend analysis, and go-to-market priorities. Adrian was able to frame our situation in ways that brought clarity to our thinking."

Sanjay Mehta
General Manager
Ricoh Innovations

"Adrian is the consummate marketing professional with a deep understanding of how to identify opportunity and build effective strategies and marketing campaigns to drive the business...I found Adrian to be a thought-leader in marketing management with a well-considered perspective that is based on years of practical experience"

Amede Hungerford
VP of Marketing
NetSuite

"Adrian has lead over a dozen difficult strategy, marketing and partnering projects that I have first-hand knowledge about, as well as dozens more that I have heard about. Do I recommend Adrian? Absolutely!"

Alan S. Michaels
Head of Research
Industry Building Blocks

"Adrian has a gift of taking complex concepts and making them intelligible and exciting."

Stanley Abraham
University Professor Emeritus
Cal Poly Pomona

"Adrian yielded impressive results through her in-depth knowledge of business that enables her to frame discussions and ask insightful questions that others may overlook. Her enthusiasm and professional approach earns the respect of senior executives."

Erna Arnesen
VP Global Channel and Field Marketing, Plantronics
Former VP, Cisco Systems

"Adrian's talk was fantastic. I am still receiving emails commenting on the value of the program."

Sheryl Chamberlain
Former Director, EMC Grassroots Innovation Program
COO – Office of the CTO, EMC Corporation
Vice President, Capgemini

"Adrian is a master at synthesizing lots of data and noise to derive insightful trends and frameworks that enlighten and create ah-ha moments for everyone. Adrian is one of the top consultants in the Silicon Valley and I recommend her highly."

Jim Chow
Head, GSI Partnerships, Americas, Google Cloud
President Emeritus and Board Member
ASAP Silicon Valley

EXPONENTIAL INFLUENCE®

DESIGNING DIGITAL HABITS

THAT ENGAGE

DISTRACTED CUSTOMERS

Exponential
Edge, Inc.®

ExponentialEdge.com
ExponentialInfluence.com

Library of Congress Control Number: 2015945469

ISBN: 978-0-9860306-2-8 (Print) 978-0-9860306-3-5 (Kindle)

14 15 16 17 18 EEI 10 9 8 7 6 5 4 3 2 1

Table of Contents

INTRODUCTION: Triggers, Technology, and Habits 1

CHAPTER 1: Peers & Power Triggers 25

CHAPTER 2: Personal Pursuit Triggers 37

CHAPTER 3: Prairie Dog Events 47

CHAPTER 4: Productivity Triggers. 59

CHAPTER 5: Price Triggers. .69

CONCLUSION: Accelerating the Customer Journey 79

ABOUT THE AUTHOR 91

INDEX 93

NOTES. 99

To My Visionary Clients and Colleagues
Who Inspire Me Everyday

INTRODUCTION

Triggers, Technology, and Habits

Whether you choose to see the MyMagic+ wristband as an ingenious technological advance or Big Brother donning Mickey ears, Disney has done it again, this time placing a billion-dollar bet on tracking visitors to their resorts and theme parks in the hopes that the data they collect will help manage crowd control, streamline the customer experience, and ultimately result in increased revenue. The candy-colored accessory allows users to enter their hotel rooms, gain admission to theme parks, and make purchases, all with a swipe of the wrist. But that's not all – it's waterproof! [1]

Disney integrates data collected from wearers of the bands with data gleaned from the My Disney Experience website and app in order to plan staffing for rides, determine the most popular souvenirs to ensure they are never out of stock, and figure out precisely how many cast members in furry suits or mermaid tails they need roaming the parks at any given moment. The early results of this pricey experiment have been overwhelmingly positive – the Magic Kingdom was able to handle three thousand more daily guests during the Christmas season in 2013 than it ever had before. Travel industry expert Douglas Quinby of PhoCus Wright calls the wristband system a "game-changer." [2]

The MyMagic+ wristband beautifully illustrates the fact that, moving forward, it will be the companies that are able to master customer time and attention that will find the most market traction. Alleviating the problem of time scarcity and the attention scarcity that necessarily accompanies it will be one of the most productive paths to gaining marketplace traction over the next decade.

The keys to accomplishing this? Digital habits and triggers. What's a trigger? And how do triggers relate to digital habits?

> _Digital Habit Tip_: A trigger is a behavioral prompt that spurs us to action and keeps us interested and engaged.
>
> _Bottom Line_: Multiple triggers lead to a habit.

Disney employs triggers masterfully because they use the information they gather about their customers for their customers' benefit – to save them time and attention. Based on customer preference data, the MyMagic+ system sends instant messages, alerting people to sudden openings for Fast Passes or reserved seating at a parade, or even a special on food or merchandise. All this enables Disney-goers, through saving them time, to squeeze as much magic as possible out of their visit: _Buy that pirate hat! Eat that Mickey Mouse ice cream! Quick, get that sidewalk seat for the Electrical Parade!_

The ways in which Disney can now trigger customers is almost limitless. If the wristband is a car, triggers are the driver that directs and accelerates it forward. Disney is not only an expert marketer, but is now an expert marketer with big data that engages customers in unprecedented ways. Since the bands are reusable, even the bracelets themselves are a memory trigger for people to return sooner than they might normally have otherwise.

Disney can now customize the guest experience based on demonstrated preferences and behaviors, making habitual engagement frictionless. *Let's go again (and spend more money). They make it so easy for us!*

According to Tom Staggs, head of the company's parks and resorts unit, the goal of the MyMagic+ wristband, is to deliver "a more immersive, more seamless, and more personal experience."[3] So don't be alarmed when Minnie Mouse is suddenly on a first-name basis with your child – it's just part of the brave new world. Disney CFO Jay Rasulo told investors that it is fully expected that this technology will have a growingly positive impact on our business in the years to come.[4] Translation:

> *This digital habit ecosystem allows Disney to access even more of their customers' time AND wallets.*

Since the band is designed to decrease the amount of time customers spend strategizing on how to get the most out of their vacation, the result will be to increase the time spent enjoying the park. And more time means more money. Retailers have long understood this concept. Consider how staples such as milk and bread are located at the back of the store while higher margin items are strategically positioned along the customer journey to entice them to linger and purchase more.

Similarly, Disney CEO Robert Iger believes the new technology will enable guests "to have a substantially better experience than they've had before because they're doing more."[5] Indeed. Spending more time with Disney – the magical time that it is for both company and consumer – will ultimately result in more meals and concessions purchased in the park. *Ka-ching!*

Tapas and Tasting Menus – Information Snacking

Engaging customers for longer periods of time is not always feasible for every brand. For most people today, time is not money; time is more important than money. With the deluge of digital devices and personal distractions, we find ourselves in a world where people snack on information.

> *Digital Habit Tip*: Cloud software subscription apps take three years on average to gain customer ROI.
>
> *Bottom Line*: Repeatable engagement and digital habits drive customer ROI.

A dispatch from the music industry from the fall of 2013 marked a major turning point when the trade magazine Variety proclaimed, "The album is dying in front of our very eyes."[6] The article was primarily a reaction to the dismal release of Katy Perry's new album, which sold a meager 287,000 copies in its debut.

The underlying idea at work here is that while everyone wants to nosh on a catchy new single from one of the reigning divas of pop music; no one wants to invest the time or attention to listen to her hour-plus statement, important as it may be to her.[7]

The fact that hype is no longer enough has been a bitter pill for music industry executives who are trying desperately to hold on to a handful of bankable stars. During the time spent paralyzed over what to do about piracy, their entire business model disappeared. They failed to recognize that we have become serial nibblers who want tapas and tasting menus, not five-course meals heavy enough to weigh us down and keep us from doing the millions of other things we could be doing.

Our collective vanishing attention span demands that things be kept short and irresistible. Shrewd companies have taken advantage of new platforms such as the video feature of Instagram and Vine (owned by Twitter), which are fifteen seconds and six seconds respectively. The six-second video has especially clicked with viewers. The short form is extremely valuable because we want to consume quickly. Brand Vines are shared four times more than other online videos and five Vines are shared every second on Twitter, indicates Heather Taylor, VP and Head of Social Content and Strategy at Ogilvy Public Relations.[8]

One of the most popular Brand Vines is Lowe's "Fix in Six" videos, which employs stop-motion animation to show quick and easy solutions to home improvement dilemmas, like how to dislodge a stripped screw or remove a sticky price tag with a blow dryer.[9]

If you think it was by accident that Vine decided on six seconds for the length of its videos, consider that a 2013 study published on StatisticBrain.com calculated the average attention span at eight seconds, down from twelve seconds ten years ago.[10] However, wait for it…

> *The attention span of the average goldfish is nine seconds.*

Yes, it is hard to believe that goldfish have a longer attention span than most people have today. New strategies need to be adopted to address the new customer reality. How do you continue to engage increasingly distracted and time-constrained customers? In order to gain traction for products and services, leading companies have learned that they must garner customer attention and time with the use of triggers and technology, triggers which prompt behavior and ultimately develop into digital habit ecosystems.

Triggers and Digital Habit Formation

Technology enhances and reinforces triggers in ways that have entered our everyday lives and our smallest behaviors. Consider the *ding*! of an arriving text message and how it prompts a familiar behavior - probably one that has become a digital habit for you: the strong urge to check your phone.

However, the possibilities extend far beyond this. What I have discovered in my work with some of the most innovative high technology companies in the Silicon Valley is that digital habits are more powerful than traditional habits – but perhaps what is more remarkable - they are quite different.

> *Digital Habit Tip*: Digital habits do not conform to a simple loop of trigger, routine, reward. Consider the difference between forming a habit to perform sit-ups everyday compared to the variety of triggers, technologies, and promotions that prompt shoppers to habitually return to Amazon's ecosystem.
>
> *Bottom Line*: Understanding the dynamics of digital habits can make or break your business.

Combining the neuroscience of human motivation and behavior with technology is the core of Exponential Influence in action. This book explores and dissects the power of triggers, technology, and habits, so you can apply their synergy to your own business. Figure I-1 depicts how triggers and technology support the customer journey and form digital habit ecosystems that we will discuss in this book.

Triggers Lead to Habit: Technology Reinforces Behavior Change

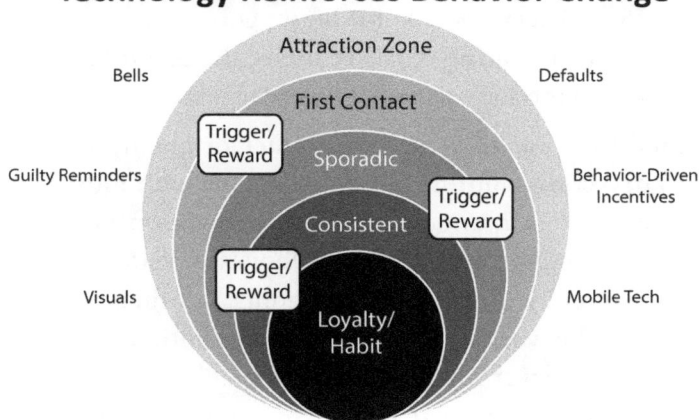

Figure I-1: Triggers Activate Customer Engagement and Habit Formation

Habit Formation

As a foundation, let's start with traditional habits. Familiar patterns and routines are what help busy people to survive and accomplish more in an economy in which time is scarce. Researchers have found that about 45 percent of our day is routine and habitual.[11,12] Without thinking about it, you get up, carry out your morning routine and get to work without a lot of conscious thought. You do it because if you had to think about every single decision such as squeezing the toothpaste tube to cracking eggs, you would be overwhelmed, exhausted, and unable to cope with the world.

We see successful products embedded into habits every day. Consider how you consume toothpaste and antiperspirant in your morning routine. A century ago, these were not goods that consumers regularly used, yet we cannot imagine leaving the house without using such products in the morning.

Corporate psychologists at consumer package companies such as P&G observe people for hours going through their daily rituals such as preparing meals or doing the laundry, looking for the opportune moment to insert a new product.

Take the case of Dryel, a product originally designed by P&G to dry-clean clothing at home.[13] A key with most habits, as we've discussed, is to understand how to fit your product into the customer's existing routine. Psychologists developed a product habit for Dryel by observing busy moms and theorized that the first wash of the week was the best place to initiate Dryel because that's when the dryer was empty and available to use the product. The first wash was a great trigger to remind the busy stay-at-home parent to use the product.

To help understand how to apply this, let's examine what psychologists call the Habit-Goal Interface Model, which is also the story of Pavlov's dog. Something triggers a habit, which is followed by a routine, and then we get a reward (or a drooling dog).

THE HABIT-GOAL INTERFACE – DRYEL

- **TRIGGER** – The first wash of the week
- **ROUTINE** – The laundry
- **REWARD** – Reduce trips to the dry-cleaner
- **"ADDICTION"** – Time and money saved

The reward is the satisfaction (and the release of dopamine), which is what makes the routine addictive. This concept was detailed in the product instructions and advertising to support development of this habit.

Similarly, have you ever seen the catch phrase "Lather, rinse, repeat" on a shampoo bottle? This is another example of how smart companies encourage customers to form habits that consume more of their products and increase sales. Habits take thinking out of the equation.

> *Digital Habit Tip*: Repetitions required to form a traditional habit depend on the difficulty of the task. One study found it could take as long as 254 days with a mean of 66 days.
>
> *Bottom Line*: The notion of twenty repetitions to form a habit is a myth.

The challenge then, lies in figuring out how to fit your product into your customer's existing routine. Although world-leading consumer companies such as P&G undertake such design into their product development as standard fare, many B-to-B tech companies spend a tremendous amount of time devising features, yet pay scant attention to designing how the new offering will fit into the business users' routine or corporate process. This design consideration should be a standard item on your go-to-market readiness checklist.

Technology Opens Up New Habit Options

What we have discussed so far are traditional habits. A New York Times reporter contacted me because he was researching an article about traditional habits and wanted to pick my brain. We discussed how companies like P&G research daily habits using psychologists and ethnographers. He then asked,

> *"Who are the top psychologists in Silicon Valley for technology products?"*

I pondered this and responded that we do not typically rely upon traditional psychologists and ethnographers like those in the consumer packaged goods industry. The people who typically study and design digital habits in Silicon Valley are user experience designers, more commonly known as UX designers. Game designers also fall into this category. These are the people who design your webpage, addictive games, and mobile app interfaces. At a strategic business level, customer experience executives, CMOs, channel executives, digital marketing and demand generation managers, oversee the design of optimal customer journeys across digital and traditional channels based on their understanding of customer habits and business processes.

With the advent of mobile, wearable sensors, and more sophisticated robotics, three types of habit options are now possible for you to apply today. Figure I-2 depicts these options on a continuum:

Habits Reduce Attention Overload:
We Offload Tasks to Brain & Computer Routines

Brain Habits	Digital Habits	Computer Routines
"Unthinking"	"Triggers and Tech"	"Set It and Forget It"

Figure I-2: Three Types of Habit Options

Brain Habits: As discussed, these are what we most often think about when we discuss habits. Traditional or brain habits govern things such as eating, commuting, and daily personal care. Such habits are etched into the limbic system of our brain and cause us to repeat activities without actively thinking about them.

Digital Habits: These also affect the brain, but technology is added to reinforce the formation of the habit and drive behavior. Digital sounds and computer routines etch such routines into the brain. Remember the familiar sound of a text or email arriving? Cues such as system bells, text messages, and pop-ups create and support habits.

Digital habits also create competitive advantage. Consider that Google has consistently maintained more than a 60 percent market share in the search market since 2009 despite Microsoft spending millions in powerhouse promotion for their rival Bing search engine. People simply are off and running on a Google search before they even think about using another tool.[14]

Indeed, in a world when customer loyalty to brands is shrinking, digital habits are very powerful engagement tools. For example, in the near future one could ask Siri (or another automated mobile phone assistant) to search for the lowest cost gas station nearby based on your daily GPS commute patterns and combine that with discount offers from local gas stations. Now imagine how the discount algorithm is devised and presented to the user and how it will trigger behavior. This leads me to an important point about digital habits and attention:

> *Rule the Decision Algorithm and You Rule the Customer*

To prove this point, consider how Google built an empire based on search engine ranking algorithms. We all know that top-ranked searches gain the lion's share of business. We can expect the digital habit trend to grow rapidly as the Internet of Things becomes a reality and wearable sensors become even more aware and predictive of our daily routines.

Computer Routines: Computer software that automates a background process helps people to cope in today's stressful world so that they can focus attention on what matters. These are tasks that people or businesses completely offload to a computer or robot in order to "set it and forget it." Computer routines do not etch onto the brain. However, change the computer routine and you've changed the habit. Consider tasks like robotic vacuums that clean our homes in the middle of the night, automated software back-ups, and online bill-paying services. Such mundane but important tasks are increasingly becoming outsourced to computers and robots as they become more sophisticated and as people are increasingly overwhelmed by too much to do. Indeed, we are rapidly advancing to the world of the Jetsons, where robots will manage our homes and complete our repetitive daily chores.

Digital Habits Are Different

Digital habits are a means to harness the attention deficit of today's 24-hour customers by utilizing technology tools to form repeatable behaviors. What struck me was the nagging question (and a reason why I wrote this book): why does a lapse in a fun, healthy exercise habit become difficult to re-initiate after stopping for a few weeks, yet shoppers who do not use Amazon for days, weeks or months are immediately drawn back into their network when they are considering a purchase? Although one could argue that exercising is not fun and that those that enjoy shopping are drawn back in, this does not account for many who despise shopping yet they easily re-engage with Amazon.

What I realized is that Amazon, and other technology leaders such as Apple, did not form such repeatable behavior through a simple Pavlovian cycle of daily repetition as we would expect with traditional brain habits. Instead they rely upon a well-designed ecosystem of triggers and technology tools that nudge the customer forward through the journey with incentives and reminders to return or buy with varying promotions and adjacent product offers. The trigger, routine, reward that we expect of a habit still exists, however the triggers will vary and the repeatable pattern will tend to occur over time rather than right away.

To illustrate the difference between a digital habit and a traditional habit consider the following: Traditional brain habits are like a race track. There is only one entrance onto the track (one trigger) but once you are on it you have one fast way around the track. Think about how you automatically tie your shoelace once you put on a shoe (trigger, routine, reward).

In contrast, digital habits are like a beltway around a city. There are multiple on-ramps with different triggers that enable entrance to the highway. Although one could get to her destination via city streets, most people use the beltway because they know it is the fastest route from point A to point B. People return to Amazon after months of no shopping because shoppers know it is the fastest way to get from A to B; they could search the Internet for other merchants but they know they can go to Amazon and get the job done faster. Different on-ramps bring people into the Amazon ecosystem: a discount offer, or a benefit such as prime shipping, or to watch a Kindle movie. Similarly to Amazon, Apple continuously adds to their digital habit ecosystem with new on-ramps such as the Apple Watch. Unlike the race track of traditional habit behavior, there are multiple triggers on-ramps that encourage people to enter into the ecosystem.

In addition, what I found is that triggers (or cues) that prompt behavior in a digital habit tend to be more emotionally driven than traditional brain habits. Consider the power of FOMO (Fear of Missing Out) and how that prompts many of us to continually check our email or phone. In contrast traditional triggers are more time or visually based i.e. it's time to brush our teeth, or we put on a tennis shoe which prompts us to habitually tie it. This leads me to another key difference:

> *Brain habits require repetition to form a habit,*
> *yet repetition can break a digital habit.*

Consider if Amazon sent you the same email day after day. You would become very annoyed and would quickly unsubscribe which would break the digital habit ecosystem relationship.

This could be caused by a neurological phenomenon researchers call sensory boredom. Dubbed the Instagram diet, one study published by Brigham Young University asked 232 participants to look at and rate pictures of food. No matter whether the subjects were given salty or sweet foods to view, researchers found that the more pictures research subjects looked at the less pleasure people got from related foods.[15]

What is novel and interesting seems to wear out its welcome more quickly with a digital habit. Perhaps this is because mobile phone bells, buzzers and other digital reinforcement tools are so strong that they easily become annoying. Figure I-3 highlights the differences between traditional brain habits and digital habits.

Digital Habits Differ from Traditional Habits

Traditional Habits
"Race Track"

Digital Habits
"Beltway"

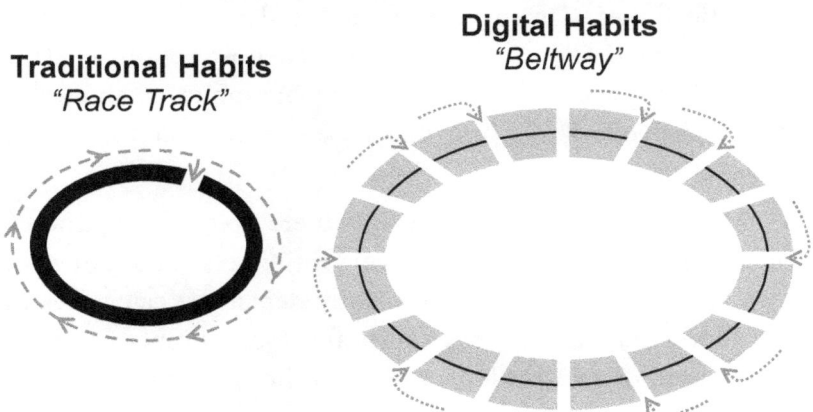

	Traditional Habits	Digital Habits
Triggers	Usually One, Same	Usually Multiple, Different
Trigger Type	Less Emotional (shoe, time-driven)	More Emotional (FOMO)
Forming	Repetition Makes Habit	Repetition Breaks Habit

Figure I-3: Traditional Habits Repeat A Simple Loop. Digital Habits Involve An Ecosystem of Triggers and Technology Tools That Drive Repeatable Behavior

Timeographics Affect Customer Decisions

The Timeographics [*pronounced* Time-o-graphics] Framework from my award-winning book, T*he 24-Hour Customer: New Rules for Winning in a Time-Starved Always-Connected Economy* (Harper Collins) helps us understand the underlying principles of how triggers, technology, and habits interact. The framework illustrates the ways in which customers triage their limited time and attention among different products and services.

As you know, we are limited by twenty-four hours of time, and about sixteen waking hours of attention every day. These constraints are depicted in Figure I-4 on the horizontal and vertical axes. Timeographics are similar to demographics as they characterize customer segments; however, instead of characterizing age and income, Timeographics characterize customer behaviors and priorities based on time and attention constraints.

Within the chart in Figure I-4, there are four quadrants: Time Magnets, Time Savers, Time Minimizers, and Time on Autopilot. These four quadrants clearly depict the categories in which our products, services and brand touch points reside in customer priorities. Let's look at each of these categories in a bit more detail.

Timeographics:
Customers Triage Offerings Into Four Categories

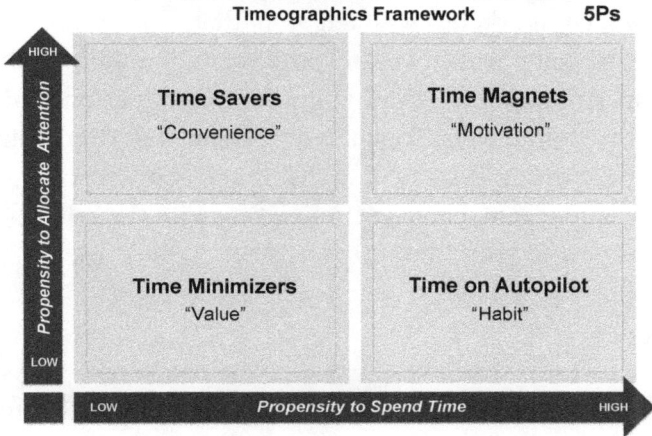

Figure I-4: The Timeographics Framework Depicts How Customers Prioritize and Behave With Time and Attention Constraints.

Time Magnets

Time Magnets are driven by human motivation and emotion. This has been the historical cornerstone of marketing practice since the 1950s. For those familiar with the TV series Mad Men, Don Draper's advertising campaigns are all about appealing to emotions: how Camel cigarettes can make you a cool person in the eyes of your friends, or a luxury-brand fragrance can automatically give you sex appeal.

Time Magnets are offerings that people are motivated to spend time with, such as careers, hobbies, or video games. Consider how some people spend countless hours interacting with friends on social media. These activities require people to spend both time and attention in order for the offering to be considered valuable.

Success in this quadrant requires that incremental value be added during each contact with the consumer. However, any experienced marketer will tell you that this is the most challenging market position for any product to maintain, as there is a constant stream of activities vying for our attention. This is why advertising often feels like an endless loop with diminishing returns to the sponsor. Instead of focusing solely on moving to or staying in this quadrant, consider innovating with the other three quadrants as part of your marketing mix.

Time Savers

Time Savers are exactly what they sound like. They target the need and desire for convenience. Customers will devote attention but not time – and that attention is usually devoted to saving time. FedEx discovered a breakthrough business model with their original advertising motto: "When it absolutely, positively has to be there overnight." Many Internet startups have created value propositions around saving the customer time. Consider how Kayak's tagline "Search one and done" emphasizes that you can access pricing for all of your travel needs across multiple travel sites, or Parking Panda, a website and app that enables you to locate, reserve, and pay for parking anywhere from large sports venues to private driveways. With Time Savers, attention is focused on how to get the task scratched off the list quickly.

Time Minimizers

In this quadrant, customers strive to devote neither time nor attention. The majority of products and services we use every day occupy this category and are primarily focused on value. There is only enough time to compare prices and a feature or two before moving on.

Time on Autopilot

This is where habits figure largely, as customers devote time but not attention. This can be a powerful position because habits are hard to break, and although people forget about them, they keep buying. Think about how much you spend each month on your Internet service subscription. A service provider such a Comcast doesn't want customers to devote attention, but to simply continue paying monthly. Time on Autopilot offerings work while we sleep. Examples include automatic bill pay services, anti-virus software, and subscription services.

With the Timeographics model in mind, we can see why customers are constantly triaging their time and attention. We all find ways to limit what we pay attention to by deploying filters. Those filters range from high-tech (Gmail's Priority Inbox) to low-tech (trusting the reviews of perfect strangers online). But our filters can easily be overwhelmed. When that happens, everything gets ignored. You can learn more about the nuances of time-value tradeoffs and time-constrained decision-making by reading *The 24-Hour Customer*.

Five Triggers That Drive Buyer Behavior

This book will share techniques that savvy companies use to engage customers and design digital habit ecosystems. My goal is to show you how to apply technology and behavior triggers in order to build Exponential Influence, resulting in your customers becoming loyal and viral brand advocates. I will also show you that you don't need to be a large company with deep pockets to make these techniques work for your business.

As the title implies, we will focus on digital habit formation to explore the brain-technology connection. Although we will discuss offloading mundane tasks to computer routines at times, the steps to developing this type of habit will not be explored in detail in this book. This book's chapters are organized around five customer buying triggers, referred to as the 5Ps.

The 5Ps

- **Peers & Power**
- **Personal Pursuits**
- **Prairie Dog Events**
- **Productivity**
- **Price**

Understanding these building blocks is essential to understanding the motivations and behaviors that redirect customer time and attention to your offering and build digital habits. Figure I-5 demonstrates how the 5P triggers relate to the Timeographics Framework.

Five Buying Triggers
That Redirect Time and Attention

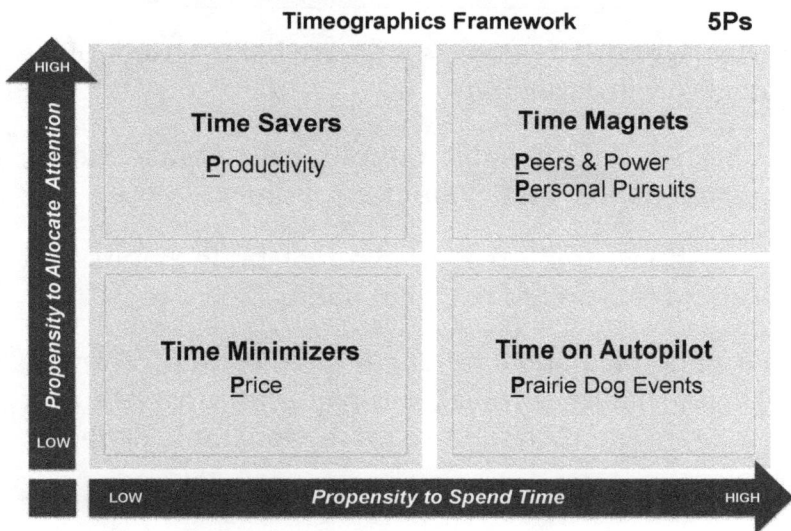

Timeographics Framework   5Ps

Time Savers Productivity	**Time Magnets** Peers & Power Personal Pursuits
Time Minimizers Price	**Time on Autopilot** Prairie Dog Events

Propensity to Allocate Attention — HIGH / LOW

Propensity to Spend Time — LOW / HIGH

Figure I-5: Triggers and Timeographics Positioning

CHAPTER SUMMARY

- Nearly HALF of people's days are habit-based. Make your product a habit.

- Three types of habit options exist: brain habits, digital habits, and computer routines.

- Repetition reinforces traditional brain habits. Yet repetition can break digital habits.

- Traditional habits repeat a simple loop. Forming digital habits involves designing an ecosystem of triggers and tech tools to drive repeatable behavior.

- Traditional habits are like a race track – simple and fast covering a limited distance. Digital habit ecosystems are like a beltway around a city with multiple on-ramps and greater distance covered.

- Triggers are a key tool to building habits and engagement.

- Design triggers and habits, not just product features.

- Timeographics matter. Customers triage products and services based on their time priorities and attention constraints.

TAKE-AWAY QUESTIONS

- Does your go-to-market readiness checklist include designing how a new offering will fit into your customer routine? What needs to change in the routine to accommodate it?

- Where does your product or service reside in the Timeographics Framework from the perspective of your customer?

- Do customer routines pertaining to your offering involve brain habits, digital habits, or computer routines?

- Is there an opportunity to apply one of the habit options (brain habit, digital habit, or computer routine process) to reinforce and sustain the relationship?

- Strategy: Can you own (or acquire) the customer decision algorithm that pertains to your offering? (There are many emerging shopping startups and decision engines that are gaining traction.)

CHAPTER 1

Peers & Power Triggers

•))

Sustaining Attention
From Royalty To Loyalty

*You are cordially invited to attend dinner
at the home of
[insert friend's name here].*

Please RSVP

Social drivers are among the most powerful triggers of all for forming digital habits. We've all experienced the pull of a *respondez vous si vous plait*. Maybe we feel put on the spot? Or perhaps a little nervous or excited. It could be that we would like to say yes, but have another obligation that evening and worry about the opportunity cost of passing up a particular invitation. The upshot is, an RSVP requires action on our part and we can only hope we are not offending our boss or circle of friends in making the right decision.

You may be surprised to know that we have none other than King Louis XIV, the legendary French Sun King and longest reigning monarch in Europe, to thank for this RSVP business. Was it instrumental to his incredibly successful reign, one which managed to avoid an overthrow of his government during a time when other European royals were frequently losing their heads? You bet! At its core, the RSVP is a form of a "guilty reminder," a technique designed to drive behavior and build habits.

By employing the RSVP, the king was in effect insisting that the nobility be present with him from his rising each morning to his retiring each night. He also threw lavish parties and galas, leaving the courtiers no time or energy to plot against him. Whenever a minister or member of the aristocracy was missing from court, the king would note it as a mark of shame and lower their status.[1]

Louis devised these guilty reminders as a method of gaining people's attention and redirecting their actions. His highness understood quite well that when people are comfortable and entertained, they essentially have no reason to leave. Why expend energy disrupting the status quo when there is a party tonight?

From Versailles to the virtual walls of Facebook, a cloud-based app, or the iPhone, creating a pleasant environment for users to spend time enables businesses to monitor behaviors. In addition, providing the next social activity within that space ensures that people don't go looking elsewhere for shopping or entertainment. The Internet of Things and emerging wearable technology will increasingly enable the promise of Timeographics to become a reality because habits and time priorities can now be easily measured. With customer Timeographic patterns mapped, new and exciting activities can be introduced at the opportune moment.

Social Motivations Drivers & Power Triggers

As the name implies, the Peers & Power trigger is based on social and status-seeking motivations. Perhaps one of the great ironies of our time-deficient lives is the fact that many people spend endless hours surfing social networks and games, competing for badges or collecting followers. We all have those friends who doggedly pursue Foursquare check-ins in an effort to become "mayor" of a business or location. One thing that hasn't changed from the Sun King's time is people prioritizing and conforming to social norms as they seek the symbols of status.

But this irony can certainly be used to the advantage of your business. Your customers' loyalty could be significantly strengthened thanks to one notable royal. Your customer doesn't always have the time to figure out the differences between your product and that of your competitors, but they will trust family and friends' endorsements. Research has found that "friends and influencers" (Peers) trigger six times more traffic and two times more conversions when they share content on social networks.[2]

Consider how Facebook markets to the mind by creating digital habits via guilty reminders, which triggers a social obligation when you see the words you have notifications pending. Could it be a friend reaching out who will feel slighted if we don't respond right away? Likewise, when we get an email from LinkedIn, we can't help wonder if there's a potentially important business contact or influential executive waiting to connect with us. What's really happening is that we're being drawn in to, and often kept, in these spaces, these businesses, through their use of the Peers & Power Triggers.

Gamification: Social Triggers on Steroids

This brings us to the topic of gamification, an ultimate digital habit ecosystem and Time Magnet. What does this buzzword really mean? Though many have claimed credit for coining the term, gamification really just means applying gaming principles to non-game experiences in order to drive desired behaviors. Although it was not called gamification at the time, King Louise XIV was a pioneer in the field – and ultimately saved his head from the guillotine. (Perhaps engaging in a real-world *Game of Thrones*?[3])

Peers & Power is about recognizing that people are willing to give their time and attention when it comes to social status involving a circle of friends or business colleagues. This places the Peers & Power trigger squarely in the Time Magnet quadrant of the Timeographics framework.

> **_Digital Habit Tip_**: **_Guilty Reminders_ are a powerful tool. To illustrate: which e-mail subject line is more powerful?**
>
> **a. Facebook [or fill in a business name] misses you, please come back!**
>
> **b. Sarah [your colleague] has posted a message for you.**
>
> **"b" would be opened more often because people care about upsetting their peer (Sarah) and not about upsetting a faceless business.**
>
> **_Bottom Line_: Leverage Peers & Power in your subject line to create a powerful trigger.**

Adobe wisely acquired Behance.com a community dedicated to showcasing and discovering creative work. What a terrific way for Adobe to nurture relationships with prospective and existing customers who use Adobe's creative software products to develop and show-off their artistic skills within this creative community. Although Behance is not set up as a game, one can see how professional one-upsmanship is at work with projects that are featured, voted-up or most viewed by the participants.

Outside of the digital realm, one recent example of marketing gamification is brought to us by our friends at Coca-Cola. Using the motto *Making a Case For Recycling One Game at a Time*, Coke launched an arcade-style game in the overcrowded and polluted city of Dhaka, Bangladesh, and now plans to roll it out in other countries. The game is designed to look like a Coke machine, but once you get up close, you see that it's a game that looks like it belongs in an arcade, not on the street corner.[4] It's called the Happiness Arcade.[5]

As soon as you reach into your pocket for coins, you realize your money is no good here. Plastic Coke bottles – inserted into a handy Coke-bottle-shaped hole – are the currency you need. When the game is over, the following message appears on the screen: Remember to take care of our environment. This sends people scrambling to find more bottles for more play. The Happiness Arcade is a terrific example of gamification with a clear purpose: It triggers a sense of social good through recycling while advertising the Coca-Cola brand. (Of course, it also makes Coke shareholders even happier if consumers buy and drink their own Coke products in order to play the game.)

Gamification Options

From a strategic perspective, the focus of any brand's approach should be to bring customers into a digital habit ecosystem that grows more useful over time. To spark your creativity, you can find a good list of game mechanic options and examples on the Gamification Wiki (www.badgeville.com/wiki/Game_Mechanics).

Even though badges were originally a core part of the Foursquare experience, they are now one of six elements used to describe users in their profiles. There are several ways that badges can support a customer journey:

Profiling: Customers self-identify their preferences and beliefs to aid in target marketing. People who add "Like" badges to Facebook for favorite foods, music, and stores give marketers the important information they need to focus their efforts. Crowd-sourced badges on LinkedIn via the Skills and Endorsements buttons are an easy way for colleagues to identify an executive's focus and skillset, making it easier for recruiters (and colleagues) to validate and understand an executive's skillset and center of gravity. Badges are a handle, similar to a tagline, which enables busy customers and executives to get a quick read on a person's interest, skills, and beliefs in a time-starved world.

Achievement: Anyone who has participated in Boy Scouts or Girl Scouts, or plays popular video games, understands the role of achievement badges: They are a mark of honor that rewards people for their efforts. However, badges are not just round patches. Well-educated people like to spout off their prestigious university credentials at cocktail parties, as a "badge" to brand a superior status. One-upsmanship and "keeping up with the Joneses" is central to the Peers & Power trigger. People spend hours pursuing higher credentials, professionally and personally. Consider how much time is spent online pursuing social media Klout scores. Once this potent motivation is understood, it can be harnessed by marketers and executives to motivate customers and employees.

Figure 1-1 identifies several gamification dimensions and options to consider in your digital habit design.

Gamification Invokes Peers & Power Triggers

Crowd-Sourced

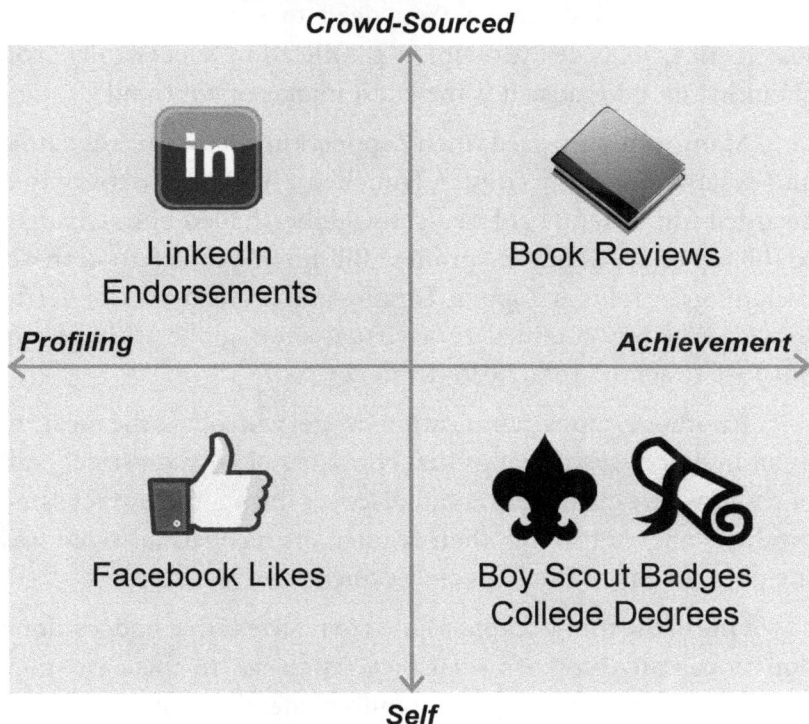

Figure 1-1: Key Badge System Design Options

Gamification Is Not A Silver Bullet

But before you throw your arms wide open to an answer to all of your company's digital woes, consider that gamification is merely a set of tools for measuring and rewarding progress. It's natural to gravitate to using game mechanics like progress bars, badges, and leader boards, but these are becoming increasingly considered overrated and passé.

It's critical to understand that games are not the same thing as gamification. Even though there are gamification vendors offering "turn-key" solutions that they claim will drive customers to act, it's not that simple. You need to have a strategy (not just tactics) in order to employ gamification successfully; you shouldn't do it because it is the latest management trend.

Many were surprised when Zappos, known for their dynamic and creative company culture, launched a VIP-only website that awarded fun, brightly colored snow globe-shaped online badges to the top of a VIP buyers' profile.[6] But no one understood these, including the folks at Zappos. Giraffes and jellyfish are wonderful in the wild, but confined to a virtual snow globe without any purpose to serve? Total head-scratcher.

Another Zappos gamification mystery involved the creation of an interactive experience that consisted of a "main street" full of shops where customers could discover links for the exact same products offered through their regular site navigation. What was the point of any of this? No one seemed to have a clue.[7]

One of the things Zappos failed to realize is that badges alone don't mean anything; it's what they represent. In this case, they didn't represent anything but random members of the animal kingdom who didn't belong in the snow.

Another dangerous trap to avoid is creating a game that no one wants to play. Marriott did just that when they launched a Facebook game called "My Marriott Hotel" to recruit for its management program. This game was a cross between Farmville and The Sims. Users could create characters with ethnicities of their choosing to populate rooms and perform different jobs, such as, hold onto your hats…buying lettuce.[8]

Strategy is especially important if advancement is involved in the game; you cannot change the rules along the way. Nothing makes players angrier than the rules changing after the game has begun. Grandfathering, long lead-times with benefits for customer transition, and transparent communications are key. Consider the uproar that occurred when airlines suddenly began changing the rules on miles required for frequent flyer redemptions.

Gamification should be specific and prescriptive. Badges and points can't miraculously revive a disengaged online community. In fact, there is such thing as "loyalty backlash," a term coined by Pug Pharm Productions CEO, Steve Bocska.[9] What Bocska refers to is active disengagement when a customer realizes that their behavior has been manipulated with no personal gain. He cites Groupon as a cautionary tale: After jumping on the initial bandwagon of the Daily Deal, which promised deep discounts, people quickly grew weary of being "rewarded" with crowds of people all trying to cash in on the same deal and unsatisfactory service from overwhelmed staff.[10]

Digital Habit Tip: Gamify your customer journey when it leads to a clear business objective and valuable customer rewards. However, do not cross the line and "game" your customers - this will quickly alienate them.

Bottom Line: Gamify but don't game your customers.

In Ivan Kuo's article "Gamification Pitfalls: Badge Fatigue and Loyalty Backlash," Bocska discusses his company's data on offering audiences a way to collect and organize things that interest them, something much more engaging than generic badges and leader boards.[11] He posits that through this approach, a user's virtual collection becomes a powerful window into their thoughts, preferences, attitudes and beliefs. Consider that fifty percent of Pinterest purchasers create a special pin board for a purchase decision.[12]

Of course gamification is not the only means to apply Peers and Power Triggers in your digital habit design. Understanding the options and pitfalls are key to striking the right balance and developing the right on-ramps to successfully engage your community.

CHAPTER SUMMARY

- Your customer doesn't always have the time to figure out the differences between your product and that of your competitors, but they will trust family and friends' endorsements.

- Friends and "influencers" (Peers) trigger six times more traffic and two times more conversions when they share content on social networks.

- Guilty Reminders are an effective digital trigger that draws upon Peer obligations.

- Power is a strong trigger in the corporate and personal worlds. People divert tremendous attention and time to improving or maintaining their reputation and status.

- Gamification is the use of gaming mechanics and elements (e.g. competition, leaderboards, and badges) to drive desired behavior and digital habits; when applied properly, it puts Peers & Power Triggers on steroids.

- Don't gamify without asking why? Understand your objectives and whether this is the best path to success.

TAKE-AWAY QUESTIONS

- Are there social triggers, such as Guilty Reminders, relating to peers (family, friends, colleagues) that could be activated around your offering?

- Are there activities that could be gamified to activate the Peers & Power trigger?

- Are there behaviors that could be rewarded in the form of advancement badges or ways to show off a skill in a professional environment such as how Adobe fosters the creative community via Behance.com?

- Are there ways to enable your customers to self-profile using badges so you can target them better?

- Can you enable crowdsourcing to profile people, such as with LinkedIn Endorsements?

- Does your organization possess the creativity, trend-spotting, organizational adaptability and agility to integrate new ideas into Peers and Power campaigns in order to sustain customer attention and keep them entertained over time?

CHAPTER 2

Personal Pursuit Triggers

•))

Fulfilling Experiences
From Malls to Magnets

*"And in the end it's not the years in your
life that count. It's the life in your years."*
– Abraham Lincoln

The windy landscaped walkways of his Southern California mixed-use shopping areas offer several roads to visitors. For some, they lead to the Apple Store for tech support, and for others, to the free yoga class held under the shade of a giant magnolia tree. Water fountains dance to Sinatra favorites and as "The Chairman of the Board" croons in the background, kids and dogs frolic on the green and a double-decker trolley rolls by.

We all know that shopping is not for everyone. Yet somehow, developer Rick Caruso has set out to prove that there is a place that offers something for everyone, that while it may be primarily for shopping, it relies on different hooks in order to offer value to many different people. Like any good fisherman knows, you need different lures for different kinds of fish.

You came to pick up a new pair of running shoes, but then you notice that staff is setting up for a free concert – and it's not amateur hour, it's a real band with a hit song that is scheduled to play that very evening under the stars. Suddenly you're calling a friend to ask them to return to the mall with you later for the live music. It's no longer a mall, it's a Time Magnet.

Appealing to our sense of fun is one of the potent forces at work in this new kind of mall that has resulted in two of the most popular and highest grossing shopping centers in the country: The Grove and The Americana.[1] Caruso has fashioned an experience that has the effect of taking each guest by the hand and walking them straight into a dream, to a place where everything sparkles, people are delightful, and no one ever wants to leave.

Dubbed the most inventive developer since Walt Disney,[2] Caruso understands the power of tapping into our need for fun and leisure, which is one of the key principles of the Personal Pursuits trigger. He has virtually exploded the old dark box of a mall and rebuilt it into a dynamic multi-layered sensory affair.

In a recent NPR Marketplace piece, Caruso says that nowadays if people have to go to an indoor mall in a pinch, they leave as quickly as possible; there's simply no reason to linger. "Everyone is so pressured with time," Caruso says. "When we do have time, we want to capture a better experience out of it."[3] Caruso sees himself in the entertainment business, referring to mall patrons as "guests" and the tenants as his customers. He doesn't seem to mind one bit if you don't spend money while you're there because he's confident that he'll "get you the next time" when you are magnetically pulled back to one of his splendid centers of commerce, as you undoubtedly will be.

Others are taking notice. A bit further south in Carlsbad, California the Westfield Group has plans underway for a $300 million dollar remodel of a forty-five-year-old mall that will begin with literally tearing the roof off the place. The concept for this project cleverly taps into the local character of the coastal town thirty miles north of San Diego, as it aims to create a "beach chic" environment.[4]

The overhaul will include adding an entirely new lineup of stores, restaurants, and lots of attractions (read: Time Magnets). "We developed a story around what we wanted to fit the community," suggests Jerry Engen, Senior VP of development, Westfield San Diego.[5] The crux of the concept centers around five zones: Ocean, Lagoon, Sandbar, Wave, and Bluff & Flats. These zones will feature a kelp-themed climbing wall, a giant aquarium, a pond, a bonfire-style fireplace, a grunion sculpture, special events venues, water walls, and tide pools.

"No longer is the standard collection of retail stores and run-of-the-mill fast food counters enough to compete for people's time and attention," writes Katherine Poythress of *The San Diego Union Tribune*.[6] Westfield is even taking things a step further than Caruso, experimenting with apps that would allow shoppers to enter information on what they are shopping for and get an inventory from merchants on their smart phones, along with the quickest route to find their Little Black Dress or "birthday gift for a five-year-old."

New technologies will continue to blur the line between online and brick and mortar channels. For example, marketing cloud software suites are providing the ability to set location "beacons" that are activated by a customer's mobile phone such as entering a store. This will automatically pass information about the customer's profile to the sales automation (CRM) system on the sales representatives' tablet so they can address the customer by name and better serve preferences such as providing a dog treat for "Lola" who has accompanied her owner to the venue.

Although the brick and mortar retail market invented the concept of dwell time, the online world is especially keen on dwell time. Firms like Nielson and Alexa keep track of metrics, such as daily time on site and page views. Such metrics are used to price the value of advertising on the site and to rank websites in order to inform and build a valuation for potential acquisition.

Whether in the physical or virtual world, where people spend time matters to companies. Leveraging the power of the Personal Pursuits trigger is key to encouraging people to spend time with you and your product.

Personal Pursuits Activate Internal Motivations

As you have likely surmised, Personal Pursuits is all about internal motivations. Similar to the Peers & Power trigger, Personal Pursuits occupies the Time Magnet quadrant of the Timeographics chart. Tapping into imagination and creating fun and pleasurable experiences for your customer are paramount. But what other factors come into play in triggering Personal Pursuits? Additional important drivers include mystery, learning, professional advancement, curiosity, and self-improvement.

Consider, for example, Williams-Sonoma hosting in-store cooking classes. Maybe you love risotto but it never comes out quite as creamy as when you first had it at that little hole in the wall in Florence. Then you happen upon a demo in Williams-

Sonoma and learn that the key to authentic sumptuous risotto is a four-hundred-dollar copper risotto pan than evenly distributes the heat so the "rice can suffer" properly as the Italians would say. Whether you buy it that day or leave there with another thing on your wish list, you wouldn't have been aware of the specialty pan that solves a long-time personal mystery without the benefit of the cooking demo.

Other examples of creating or increasing dwell time are seen with companies such as Guitar Center offering weekly recording sessions and of course Apple, with its free workshops and Genius Bar. In both these instances, providing expert insight and technical support the customer can't get anywhere else is a fantastic tool for getting people to stay with you and return again and again. There are many ways to create a learning environment, from in-store videos, to make-up artists doing demos to show off beauty products.

In the B-to-B arena professional development and advancement is another way to trigger Personal Pursuits driven habits. Adding value could also be as simple as uncovering information that is relevant to your customers' businesses and sharing it with them as a trend line. For example, you might provide a free report on benchmarks in your industry based on your aggregated customer data. As long as the business continues to use your service, you will continue to offer the trend information; if they switch to a competitor then the data is lost or you can charge for access.

Tapping Into Mystery and Curiosity

In the arena of mystery and curiosity, a good example is an online game such as www.geoguessr.com that has become very popular. Triggering curiosity by creating mystery taps into the Time

Magnet quadrant. We all enjoy the suspense involved with solving a mystery or figuring out a "whodunit."

Although treasure hunts are nothing new, GPS takes them to a new level. There are now nearly a million geocaches worldwide, according to www.geocaching.com, hidden everywhere from the corners of Manhattan high-rises to forests of the Sierra Nevadas. These treasures are usually the size of an index card, placed by enthusiasts, and found by seekers using GPS and the geocaching website. Typically there is an assortment of trinkets and the seeker is asked to take one and leave another so the game can continue.

> *Digital Habit Tip*: **Combine your physical location(s) with the virtual world to create a treasure hunt concept.**
>
> *Bottom Line*: **It's a great way to incent prospective customers to visit your location or learn more about your business**

The treasure hunt concept opens endless possibilities. The band Coldplay is using the idea to promote their new album Ghost Stories with a hunt that directs its Twitter followers to find lyric sheets handwritten by front man Chris Martin that have been hidden in ghost story books in libraries around the world. One of the envelopes even contains a Golden Ticket giving the finder and a guest a free trip to London to see Coldplay live at Royal Albert Hall.[7]

Victoria's Secret is another brand that has also enjoyed great success with its mobile initiatives that build on past efforts with image recognition and collection. Through its Pink Nation app, the first one hundred customers to locate, snap a photo of the given Victoria's Secret image and upload it, receive a free gift. The campaigns are easily updated and swapped out for seasons and holidays.

In another example, the NBA also launched its H-Town Playoffs Digital Scavenger Hunt this year. The game instructs fans to take photos wearing their Rockets gear at specified Houston locations, post the photo using the hashtag #HTown, and then meet in front of the Toyota Center at a given time to receive one raffle ticket per post to win playoff tickets.

> ***Digital Habit Tip***: Platforms such as FourSquare and Facebook pages enable low-cost ways for customers to "discover" your brand in the form of free samples and "puzzler of the week" questions with giveaways to the winner.
>
> ***Bottom Line***: You don't need to have a large marketing budget to activate Personal Pursuits. Just creativity and energy to execute.

Think your B-to-B business is too boring for a treasure hunt? Think again. A small business accounting agency runs a "question of the week" puzzler on their Facebook page called, "Is it deductible?" They ask their community an interesting question every week, such as whether a family that incurs high costs of transporting their Great Dane is deductible if the family had to move to take on a new job.

Feeling Better About Ourselves

No discussion of Personal Pursuit drivers and motivation would be complete without mentioning self-improvement. Facebook's recent acquisition of Moves, the fitness/activity tracker that will operate much like WhatsApp and Instagram, (without Facebook branding) will enable Facebook to track user activity through sensors built into devices such as accelerometers. That data is then translated into user-friendly stats, such as steps taken and calories burned.[8] Ah, the never-ending personal pursuit of burning calories.

Charitable giving to those less fortunate is another area that makes people feel better about themselves. We feel good when we support a cause. For some, such acts co-mingle with the Peers & Power trigger as donors enjoy showing-off their generosity at charitable auctions or by adorning a university building with their name after funding with a sizable donation.

CHAPTER SUMMARY

- Personal Pursuits are motivators that are intrinsic to the individual. This trigger can include elements of:
  - Fun
  - Imagination
  - Mystery
  - Self-improvement
  - Charitable Giving

- Personal Pursuits are a powerful Time Magnet that increase customer dwell time and repeat engagement with your offering; more time means more money.

- Providing consistently high value that satisfies an underlying motivation relative to the time invested is a critical element to success with Personal Pursuits.

- Mystery and treasure hunt concepts deliver the thrill of seeking out and capturing "treasure," whether it is in the form of a free ice cream or hand-written lyrics from your favorite rock band.

TAKE-AWAY QUESTIONS

- Can any element of Personal Pursuits be applied to your marketing efforts? Are there activities that could activate social good or self-improvement in the trigger?

- Customers will be sensitive to whether an offering is delivering sufficient value for their time and attention. Make sure you ask: Have we earned their time?

- Is the motivation strong but short-lived, as often happens with those whose interest is piqued by a new fad? If so, what is your next step or next on-ramp to keep the customer engaged?

- What kind of low-cost high-value rewards can you offer? Do you have excess capacity in the form of unpurchased seats or inventory that would be highly valued by your prospects and drive personal pursuits to acquire them?

CHAPTER 3

Prairie Dog Events

•))

From Burrowing to Bolting

"We are what we repeatedly do." – **Aristotle**

Do you remember the Netflix horror from a few years back? Not when you were watching the latest scary flick, but when the company itself became the horror show by abruptly increasing their monthly subscription price by a whopping 60 percent?

Although this may have seemed like a simple operational pricing decision, the company risked everything with this ill-conceived move, nearly doing more damage than *Friday the 13th's* Freddy Krueger and Jason combined. The next plot twist unleashed another classic movie trope: the angry mob. At the height of this mess, Netflix CEO Reed Hastings even earned himself the unflattering nickname on social media, Greed Hastings, and wound up unwittingly starring in his own real-life movie.[1] We'll call it *Apocaflix*. The following is just one of the choice e-mails the company received from irate subscribers:

Dear Netflix,

Nice work, [doggie] bags! I used to love Netflix and have recommended it to all of my friends and family. What is the justification for raising my cost 60% and passing it off as a "terrific value"? Time for me to check out the competition. How dare you.

Your Once Loyal Customer[2]

Cut to one year later and Netflix executives were still apologizing. Despite continued fails, such as listing Anne Frank: The Whole Story in the comedy section until another exasperated subscriber pointed it out for the worldwide web,[3] there was one thing working in the company's favor: They happened to be in a market that was growing by over 100 percent as consumers continued to make the switch from physical DVD rentals to streaming content.[4]

In the seven quarters leading up to the price hike, Netflix added at least one million subscribers. Then in Q3 of 2011, the ire that was unleashed resulted in 810,000 defectors.[5] What the Netflix tragedy represents is the trigger we call a Prairie Dog Event.

Perhaps the best way to define a Prairie Dog Event is to return to the words from the angry Netflix customer quoted above:

> *"Time for me to check out the competition."*

One day, we are underground, happily burrowing like a prairie dog, and then something happens to wake us, shake us, and pop us out of our hole in a panic to look around for a better deal.

The good news is there are two sides to a Prairie Dog Event. Clearly, Netflix was on the losing side in this example, while their competitors (temporarily) had the advantage. Other common types of Prairie Dog Events are:

- **A computer breaks down. You think:** *Maybe it's time for me to switch brands and get all new software.*
- **A poor customer service experience. You think:** *I'll show you what happens to people who put me on hold for forty-five minutes!*
- **An auto recall. You think:** *My family's not safe in this vehicle anymore and I just saw an ad for Brand X, which is running a great lease deal.*
- **Life stage events. You think:** *Oh my gosh, I'm having a baby and they require lots of stuff. Or maybe it's: I'm going to buy a home. I'll need insurance with that. Or sticker shock hits home: My firstborn is going off to college and judging by the price tag it seems that dorm rooms are now made out of pure gold. I'm going to need a home equity line of credit.*

Prairie Dog Triggers Arise When Habits or Computer Algorithms Break

The Prairie Dog Event trigger fits in the Habit/Autopilot Quadrant of the Timeographics Framework since we all typically remain on autopilot with things we like to "set and forget" such as subscriptions, automatic bill payment processes, and buying the same familiar brand until something shakes things up and causes us wake up and look around to switch to a competitive offering.

In B-to-B, business processes are typically engineered into steps that are fossilized into compliance procedures, employee training, and software. This is why change is so difficult in corporations. Habits, no matter whether they are brain- or computer-driven, are a powerful force that can work in your favor if you are the incumbent and customers are kept satisfied with processes that work for them.

However, that is a BIG IF, according to a new report from IBM that finds many marketers are failing to maintain a good customer experience. According to Katie Ingram for CMS Wire, IBM's The State of Marketing study found that "$83 billion is lost in marketing each year due to a poor customer experience and only 20 percent of those surveyed reported having good customer experience skills."[6]

Most of the time, what makes the difference between a customer who stays and one who goes is a personal level of engagement that extends across multiple or omni-channels namely social media, service lines, in-store, and mobile. This is an emerging complex challenge for today's CMOs.

Defaults and Habits Prevail When Time Is Scarce

People are often reluctant to make any kind of change as they fiercely guard their time and attention; habits are a means to save time and energy because they do not have to think. As discussed in the introduction, about 45 percent of our day is habitual. Back in 2002, Google reached a deal with AOL for fifty million dollars in advertising to become AOL's default search engine. Today, it is estimated that they pay one hundred million dollars for the same arrangement with Mozilla.[7]

For behavioral economists, psychologists, and marketers, defaults are part of a rich study that explores "decision architecture" – how a choice is presented or framed, writes Steve Lohr for The New York Times. Defaults are great because they make the decisions for us, whether they are relatively unimportant ones like which search engine to use, or critical ones that affect our future, such as participating in a retirement plan that automatically draws from our paycheck.

Consider how websites often present consumers the one-year subscription option instead of the cheaper one-month option as a default. Have you ever noticed how they label a more expensive, upgraded option as "most popular?" Perhaps it is "most popular" with the company's investors who prefer that option for its profitability therefore it is set as the default on their ordering menu. Most customers do not question what "most popular" really means.

Additionally, you have also probably seen e-commerce sites that ask you to opt-out (uncheck the box) versus opt-in (check the box) to add you to their newsletter and promotion list when you buy. These are great examples of defaults that form digital habits.

Defaults frame digital habits. In a time-strapped economy, people often favor the fast choice instead of expending the energy involved in making a non-default choice. This is an integral part of a Time-Value trade-off decision discussed in my book, *The 24-Hour Customer.*

Of course, you need to be careful not to overdo defaults as consumers will get upset about opt-out versus opt-in choices. We saw this with the sensitive topic of Facebook's privacy policy pertaining to sharing user profiles a few years ago.

Changing Habitual Behavior

Having the ability and the willingness to change is not always enough to alter behavior. A trigger must be involved to prompt an action that shifts a customer's behavior. If your goal is to attract new customers and build digital habits for offerings that reside in the Time on Autopilot Timeographic in the minds of customers, then you need to be on the lookout for Prairie Dog Events with your competitors. It is at these triggåer points that you and your competitors are most vulnerable. Social media comments and online customer reviews are a great way to identify people who are "prairie dogging." Once found, how do you catch a potential customer who is prairie dogging?

> ***Digital Habit Tip***: Most harried customers will choose a default you provide. Such defaults can be set in your favor.
>
> ***Bottom Line***: Utilize defaults to drive desired behaviors and create no-brainer decision-making for customers to complete a transaction.

Two Ways to Catch a Prairie Dog

1) Wait for them to pop up and be ready to offer enticing alternatives while they are looking around and you have their attention.

2) Smoke them out! This involves disrupting customer behaviors by offering exponential value.

In early 2014 AT&T began offering a $450 credit to T-Mobile customers for switching service plans in the U.S. This was intended to smoke prairie dogs out of their burrows by offering significant credit to offset early termination charges and provide an upgraded device. Once customers switch, of course the hope is that they remain and form a repetitive purchasing habit.

In the US, deep discount Triple Play Bundles (phone, TV, Internet) were created to make switching providers even more difficult and time-consuming, thereby keeping customers from leaving because it's just too much hassle. Many customers annually call their providers to get the latest promotional pricing for a twelve-month contract. However, there are many customers who don't and wind up paying a premium until something breaks or they read the bill and find their promo expired and they have been paying full fare.

> *Digital Habit Tip*: Utilize social media monitoring tools to identify dissatisfied customers of your competitors.
>
> *Bottom Line*: Be ready to approach them with your offering because the customer may be ready to switch.

A surprising recent example of prairie dogging that was detailed in Wired Magazine comes from the auto industry. According to Tesla's own data, they sold 22,477 Model S sedans in 2013. Conventional wisdom would likely lead you to believe that these buyers were historically the owners of other luxury vehicles, but that's where you'd be mistaken. Many more of them owned another electric car before their Tesla, a Toyota Prius to be exact. Most Tesla buyers want the benefits of an electric vehicle. However, well-heeled Prius owners were "smoked out" of their comfortable Prius nest when the Tesla came along with exceptional amenities and style, items not offered on the spartan Prius. According to a Polk Automotive analyst, the Model S is acquiring owners of Toyota vehicles more frequently than any other brand. Of those, Prius defectors lead the way.[8]

But perhaps the most compelling example of smoking out prairie dogs is Amazon Prime. Amazon had already created a habit with customers in that for many consumers today, the purchasing process begins with checking the Amazon price. Enter Amazon Prime, a membership program offering free two-day shipping. Membership has doubled in less than two years and is expected to double again by 2017. A report published by Morningstar and

Consumer Intelligence Research Partners estimates that Amazon Prime now has ten million members.[9] (Just imagine the numbers when delivery drones become ubiquitous and things can show up on your doorstep within hours. How's that for instant gratification?)

The creators of Amazon Prime projected that it would break even in two years. Imagine their delight when it only took three months. Talk about a digital habit. Customers couldn't get enough of the fast free shipping and spent 150 percent more after becoming Amazon Prime members, which in and of itself cost them seventy-nine dollars. Amazon Prime changed their behavior because they began buying things they never used to on Amazon to save themselves time and trips to the store. Robbie Schwietzer, VP of Amazon Prime indicated that he doesn't remember anything that has been as successful at getting customers to shop in new product lines.[10] If Amazon has its way, no one will want to shop anywhere else ever again.

An Amazon Prime member now makes $1,224 in purchases per year, compared to a non-member Amazon shopper, who averages $505 annually.[11] Make something free and suddenly consumers don't think it's so valuable anymore.[12] In 2014, Amazon raised the Prime Membership fee to ninety-nine dollars and added a few more benefits, such as a library of free music downloads.[13] With the frictionless ease-of-use and convenience of Amazon, most users are expected to remain in the program to gain maximum ROI on the free shipping.

So what is the key to designing an addicting habit-based program like Amazon Prime? It begins with ensuring that everything runs smoothly while quietly adding value that deepens the relationship. Bankers often call this approach the "Magic

Seven": Once a customer signs up for seven services, such as bill pay, checking or savings accounts, etc., best practice data shows that they will own the customer for life. This is why banks like Wells Fargo continually offer lucrative promos and incentives to sign customers up for additional services.

Digital Habit Tip: The relationship with the customer does not stop at the sale. Make on-boarding frictionless

Bottom Line: Cloud businesses have only a 10% chance of a customer becoming a reference if not satisfied in 90 days (rule of thumb).

It is important to understand that unlike the sales process, a habit development process does not stop the day the customer places the order; it continues until the customer is fully functional and has adopted your product into their routine, whether it is a brain habit or business process.

CHAPTER SUMMARY

- Prairie Dog triggers are based on a disruption of a habit or process. Such triggers could also be calendar events, like end-of-year deadlines.

- There are two sides to a Prairie Dog tale: Avoid anything that would cause your customers to pop their heads up and check out the competition, but also be on the look-out for Prairie Dogs looking for a competitive offering.
  - Monitor customers commenting about your competitors on social media so that you can react quickly.

- There are two ways to catch a Prairie Dog who is currently buying from your competitor:
  - Wait for them to become dissatisfied so that they pop up to look around, or
  - Smoke them out by offering exponential value.

- Providing exceptional customer service and avoiding computer or process hiccups is one of the best ways to protect against Prairie Dog Events.

- Cultivating and deepening the customer relationship through cross-selling more offerings is another key to maintaining stability. This deepens the burrow, thus making it more time-consuming to dig out and switch.

TAKE-AWAY QUESTIONS

- Can you list Prairie Dog Events for your prospective customers? What are the events and incidents that could cause customers to defect or change the way they approach a habit?

- Is your team able to quickly identify and respond to Prairie Dog Events with your existing customers? Is your team empowered to act?

- Does your team have visibility via social media analytics into Prairie Dog events created by your competitors? Are they empowered to quickly jump on these opportunities?

- What are ways you can extend value to your customers to deepen the relationship into a habit or embed into a business process to make it more effort to switch?

CHAPTER 4

Productivity Triggers

From Pain to Gain

"Lost time is never found again" – **Benjamin Franklin**

You're on a first date or maybe it's your twentieth wedding anniversary and you're off to the opera in a major city. You've already plunked down way more money than you would like to admit for those playoff tickets or Puccini. Dinner before the main event ran you over a hundred bucks, not including the wine, and you've been planning this night for weeks, down to the last detail. So when you get stuck in an epic traffic jam that makes you late to the venue, your dreams of the perfect evening are dashed because there's nowhere left to park!

But all is not lost if you have a smartphone and reside in a major city. Thanks to innovation and technology, there are now many apps that will find parking for you in real time. Some of these apps are free, some inexpensive, but all are priceless. Why? They increase our productivity. They move us from pain to gain, saving us lots and lots of precious time. The prospect of saving time is a key way to incent people to change their habits and routines.

The parking associated with these apps can be found in lots, garages, and even private driveways. Some companies encourage you to list your own spot in return for a 20 percent commission. VoicePark (www.voicepark.org) in San Francisco gives you turn-by-turn directions to the closest open parking space, claiming that they have reduced the time it takes to find parking from 6.5 minutes to 45 seconds.[1] 'Can I Park Here?' is a New York City app that lets users upload a photo and have the cryptic language of parking signs interpreted for them, giving them the official word on whether they can park in that spot with impunity. In some cities notorious for towing and impounding, this could mean a savings of over four hundred dollars.

ParkMe tracks more than twenty-eight thousand locations worldwide and Parkopedia is linked to twenty-six thousand lots in North America, so it should come as no surprise that automakers are getting in on the act. Audi has partnered with ParkMe to add the app's services to their dashboard and Parkopedia announced in late 2013 that they have a deal with Volvo to offer embedded parking information for the drivers of their cars.[2] The brand best known for making one of the safest cars on the road is now also one of the easiest to park.

In a New York Times article, Casey Jones, VP of Institutional Services at Standard Parking, says that what used to be just about parking cars has now become a service industry.[3] What this means is that sharing apps such as Uber and Airbnb are examples of how Internet platforms enable access to underutilized assets that can now be monetized to aid consumers in their quest for increased productivity.

> *Digital Habit Tip*: Do you have under-utilized assets in your business, such as empty seats or unused inventory that could be parsed and shared across users by applying technology?
>
> *Bottom Line*: There is a "land-grab" going on as the sharing economy emerges.

Of course, it is important to own the assets you are selling. Rome-based startup Monkey Parking created an app that enabled drivers to notify parking seekers when they were leaving a spot so they could auction off the space in congested San Francisco. The monkey wrench came when it was determined that Monkey Parking was auctioning off public parking spaces on city streets. Consequently, the City of San Francisco ordered the fledgling startup to shut down.[4]

Monkey Parking claimed they were syncing up parkers and selling the notice that a driver was leaving and not selling the space itself. Umm… right. The City didn't buy their claim either. I'll bet that we will see next-generation parking apps pivoting to a business model that provides a significant revenue share to the city. Then the city will be all for such apps because this will fill parking tax coffers with minimal investment, and maximize parking receipts and utilization.

If you happen to be unlucky enough to get a parking ticket there's an app for that too, at least in San Francisco, and there's one on its way in Chicago. It won't help you if you jumped a curb or blocked a fire lane, but if there's any gray area and you think you have a case? Use the app Fixed (www.getfixed.me) to upload documentary photos – the broken meter, the confusing signage, the faded paint on the curb - and you just might come out unscathed. This app even shows you the probability for beating your ticket based on location and previous cases.[5]

Redirecting Attention by Offering to Save Time

The Productivity Trigger occupies the Convenience Quadrant in the Timeographics Framework because it is about saving time and increasing productivity. Consider if I told you I could help save you three hours a day – that would get your devoted attention, right? This is because everyone wants to learn how to become more productive. This is the power of the Productivity trigger in developing digital habits.

Many Internet startups innovate online services in this space. Consider Instagram, the company that Facebook bought for a cool billion. What makes it so valuable? Perhaps it's the fact that it created a new habit that also saves us time. What was once a time consuming ordeal – to upload and share photos – has now been transformed into instant gratification and makes anyone look like a fine arts photographer with its fancy filters and frames. Snap a shot on your phone and immediately share it with your social network. Next!

Another great example in the transportation sector that makes brilliant use of the Productivity trigger is the startup AirHelp, which assists air travelers in recouping from an airline when their flight has been delayed, overbooked, or canceled. Who knew there was such big money to be made in this arena? According to AirHelp, only one tenth of a percent of eligible passengers claim their compensation because let's face it; no one has the time to fight City Hall.[6]

**Digital Habit Tip**: Link related tasks together into a path for users, such as uploading photos, auto-filling a request, and including GPS info to encourage ease of adoption.

**Bottom Line**: Simple touch points for users with mobile apps save time interacting with your company, which encourages more engagement because customers do not view it as a hassle.

For an overbooked, delayed, or canceled flight in the US, you could be looking at collecting up to thirteen hundred dollars or eight hundred dollars for a flight to Europe,[7] which is why the airlines make it so very difficult for you to recover. How exactly does it work? Initially, a customer would go to the website (www. getairhelp.com) to enter their information and find out how much they would be able to claim. Recently, however, the service has been refined and now users are able to connect through a Gmail account to allow AirHelp access to search your flight activities up to three years back, which is the window of time you have to make a claim.

As promising a prospect as it is for recovering some serious coin, we're back to the problem of time – a fact airlines are well aware of and use to their advantage. "If passengers attempt this process themselves, they'll have to send tons of documents, they'll experience dead links. And if you get through that hurdle, you're likely to be rejected by the airline saying that it's an extraordinary circumstance," AirHelp CMO Nicolas Michaelsen told a group at the Disrupt NY 2014 conference. "We auto-generate the legal documents that you should send to the airline."[8] In essence, the app is a hoop eliminator.

What does AirHelp receive for their trouble? A 25 percent cut, but only if they recover for you. This doesn't really seem like that much when you consider that you were unlikely to recover anything without their intervention. It's also why the company has been making revenue since day one and will turn profitable within a month or two. So far, twenty-five thousand people have used the service.[9]

Then there's healthcare. Good old-fashioned, overly complicated, super-inflated American-style healthcare. This is a sector practically screaming out in pain (the diagnosis is clear but there's still no cure) for more convenience. Walgreens seems to be taking the lead here with the rollout of about four hundred Take Care Clinics within the drugstore's existing locations. The goal is to streamline the healthcare visit while delivering incredible value and transparent pricing. They offer services in three major areas:

- **Prevention & Wellness** – Vaccines, physicals, and screening.

- **Treatment** – Illnesses, minor injuries, skin conditions.

- **Monitoring & Management** – Overseeing ongoing and chronic conditions such as asthma, diabetes, high blood pressure and high cholesterol.

The concept of the retail clinic has incredible appeal in that it offers unparalleled convenience and repeat engagement opportunities through better access to care with longer hours and more locations than our beleaguered healthcare system now provides. Not everyone in the medical profession applauds these efforts, however, especially groups like the American Association of Family Physicians. Their concerns are based on the ever-increasing role of non-doctors in these types of settings, which are typically run by physician's assistants and nurse practitioners. Despite these protests, the Byzantine healthcare system is overdue for its check-up.

But for the ultimate in medical convenience, make your way to Medicast.com for house call doctors on demand, twenty-four hours a day. House calls are making a huge comeback because it just doesn't get any more convenient. Think about it. The doctor can't very well make you wait when they are in your house. In productivity terms, you just gained back the transportation and waiting time you would have spent going to the doctor's office by using this service. Not to mention the fact that you didn't expose yourself to any unnecessary germs at a medical office or hospital.

Dubbed the "Uber for healthcare," the company has enjoyed great success in Miami and is now expanding to other cities. The website touts the ability to "hail a doctor," who will be on the doorstep of your home, office, or hotel in two hours or less. The price for this convenience is between $199 and $249 depending on the city. There is even a movement underway for some people to keep insurance for catastrophic occurrences and cut the insurance companies out for their more routine medical care. Medicast doesn't deal with insurance companies, so they have essentially cut out the middleman as well.

Considering that this is significantly less than a trip to the ER, it may not be a luxury at all. "In theory, Medicast will allow doctors more freedom to manage their schedules, see fewer patients, and conduct more humane appointments – all while potentially running a more lucrative practice," according to Killerstartups.com.[10] Seems everything old is new again when it comes to saving time.

CHAPTER SUMMARY

- The Productivity trigger is all about saving time. It is a key way to redirect attention to your offering.

- By definition, convenience-driven products are practical. What they offer is a time savings, whether that is part of the product itself or through the purchase or delivery.

- When developing convenience-driven products, focus on eliminating steps, reducing time, and giving customers choice and control over their time.

- Underutilized assets offer a great way to apply market-sharing apps to sync buyers with sellers. Just make sure you own the rights to the asset. (Remember Parking Monkey and the City of San Francisco.)

- Conveniences are not habits, though habits are convenient.

TAKE-AWAY QUESTIONS

- Can your offering provide superior convenience that matters to your customers? How sustainable is this time-saving relative to new entrants?

- Can you quantify time savings for your customer to make the benefit tangible and activate the trigger? For example, "This will save your team x amount of hours."

- What are ways to reduce search time, purchase time, and/or consumption time for your offering?

- Do you have underutilized assets that could benefit from sharing apps?

- Does your organization have the logistical and operational excellence to deliver consistently and on time to keep your customers from waiting?

CHAPTER 5

Price Triggers

·))

From Discounts to Devotion

"The 10 Commandments contain 297 words.
The Bill of Rights is stated in 463 words.
A recent federal directive to regulate the
price of cabbage contains 26,911 words."
– Unknown

The Holiday Pricing Shuffle. It sounds like a dance and it pretty much is: It's the elaborate show that retailers put on not just for the holidays (but also for much of the rest of the year nowadays) in the never-ending pageantry of undercutting.

One a recent Black Friday promotion, Amazon dropped its price on a different dance – a game called Dance Central – to $24.99 in order to match Best Buy's door-buster special and then dropped it again to $15 when Wal-mart attempted to hip-check everyone else off the stage. Amazon answered with a two-step of sorts: raising and lowering their price once a day for a week. According to Stephanie Clifford in her New York Times article, "Retail Frenzy: Prices on the Web Change Hourly," the unluckiest buyer paid more than triple the price that the luckiest buyer paid.[1] But at the end of the day, this can be a line dance of death.

> *Digital Habit Tip*: **Technology enables behavioral pricing based on digital customer behaviors and clicks.**
>
> *Bottom Line*: **If your customer is scanning mobile barcodes, chances are they are comparing prices while standing in a retail store. Timing discounts is important.**

There are myriad risks associated with competing on price alone. Buyers are beginning to realize that they may not be able to trust the price they're getting because it is so likely to change. Even still, it's tempting for retailers to go this route because when their price is the lowest, they can increase sales volume, which means they dominate in price comparison tools. Part of this strategy also sometimes involves cutting prices to force the competition into a losing price and deplete its inventory. Then they wait for the competitor to sell out and jump back in the game. But the battle to become the low-price leader is most certainly a short race to the bottom.

There's no doubt that price is one of the most heavily utilized triggers by businesses but it often develops into bad habits for buyers that expect a discount with every transaction. Everyone wants to come away from a purchase with the feeling that they have gotten the best deal. For some, it's a game: How much can you negotiate and brag to your friends at the next party? For others it is an imperative: There's only so much in the budget to spend.

There are two ways to approach the Price trigger for your business. The question is:

> *Do you use price as a spice or as an entree?*
>
> - **As a Spice**: To be used sparingly to incent the sale as part of a campaign that primarily relies on other triggers such as Peers & Power.
>
> - **As an Entree**: Your company's value proposition to the customer is based on providing the best value and organized around being the low-cost leader.

Price is such a powerful trigger that many companies confuse these two approaches and fail to form meaningful habit ecosystems. Unlike other triggers where too much repetition breaks habits, too much discounting will repeatedly engage customers but will break your bank account. The routine will be broken as soon as your competitor comes along with a better deal.

When your business occupies the Value Quadrant of the Timeographics Framework (see Figure I-4 on page 17) and serves up price as an entree, it is important to realize that your customer is a bargain shopper. However, if you are using price as a spice, your customers will typically be attracted to additional qualities in your business that will cause them to respond to other triggers. It's also quite possible that you need to identify more clearly who your customers are (or who the customers you want are) and adjust your marketing to target those who are likely to respond to the differences you offer and are willing to pay slightly more for a better value or personalized service.

Price as a Spice

If it makes sense for your business to use the price spice, remember that seasonings are additive, and ideally, it should be sprinkled on top of something else – in this case another trigger. One way to do this is to add the *spice of value* to your offering. Think of auto dealerships that offer free car washes for the car you purchased or leased through them. This isn't something that's part of the sales pitch; it's just a value-added element that is good for the customer as much as it is for the brand that would prefer their cars look great on the road. In the meantime, they are developing a customer habit to return again and again to the car lot, where the latest models are on display.

> *Digital Habit Tip*: A discount at the end of a sales process with a limited-time offer can seal the deal.
>
> *Bottom Line*: Sprinkle price sparingly on top of other triggers.

Another example of a spice of value comes from an idea adopted in the world of CPAs, in which an accountant hosts a seminar on various financial topics, including the Affordable Care Act (yes, there are people who have read all 906 pages of it). These kinds of seminars generate lots of referrals for the CPA, as everyone who attends them raves about it afterwards to their friends and family. When people trust a brand, they do the work for you. In this instance, the final close can be made with a special email discount for services. So the price spice is sprinkled atop triggers such as Peers & Power or Productivity that got the prospect there in the first place.

Creating scarcity is another price spice. When you put out the word that your offer will end soon or only offer a limited number of a particular item, you are making it extra spicy! Whatever the reason, we humans place a higher value on an object that is scarce than on one that is in ample supply. Clearly, this is the force at work with the Black Friday phenomenon, as consumers thrive on the competition for so-called limited items. This would be an example of dusting the price spice on top of the Personal Pursuits trigger, which plays on the competitive impulse.

Price as an Entree

Now let's say that you want to use the Price trigger as an entree. Improving efficiency is one option on this menu that allows businesses to stay competitive in the Value Quadrant. Southwest Airlines was the first to use electronic ticketing, not to mention they get their planes back in the air an average of twenty minutes after landing, while other airlines take two to three hours.[2] It is practices like these (along with a loyalty program) that have made Southwest one of the most profitable airlines in the industry. They have created a customer habit that has many customers checking Southwest's portal first for low-priced airfare.

Niche Markets

Another way to avoid competing on price alone is to create a niche within a broader market. Think of the auto repair shops that specialize in German cars. As a specialist, they don't have to compete with every garage in town. In this way, they can make a healthy profit while delivering a valuable service.

Paula Long, CEO of DataGravity, knew she wasn't interested in being a small fish in a big pond, so she created her own pond:

"small to medium-sized businesses with self-serve, big-data solutions rather than large companies with highly customized solutions that attract the competition," writes Forbes Magazine.[3]

Long raised forty-two million dollars in venture capital by targeting a niche within a large and lucrative market. She saw the problem smaller businesses have with big data solutions being too expensive and complicated. Large companies have data science teams in-house, but this is out of reach for most smaller guys, so Long's company set out to design self-service analytics. One of the beta testers for some of DataGravity's tools is a group of teachers and administrators who are able to get real-time information on the learning processes of students.

Pricing Overuse Leads to Unprofitable Buying Habits

All this is not to say that keeping prices in check is necessarily a bad thing. The Price trigger occupies the Value Quadrant of the Timeographics framework, which can be a competitive position to hold IF your offering is specifically designed to work as an "entree." The problem is, even though price can trigger a change in behavior, it's typically only going to hold a customer's attention for a short time. Pricing often isn't set up to be a habit and tends to be a one-time deal that ends with people refocusing their attention elsewhere after they've benefited from your generosity. Loyalty programs that incentivize repeat purchases go further toward the formation of customer habits and ongoing engagement with price as a trigger.

"Low price shoppers are loyal to price, not to you," writes Rhonda Abrams for Inc.com.[4] When the competition decides to squeeze you hard with rock bottom prices, your customers disappear as quickly as you were able to win them over with that initial great deal. The price game becomes a vicious cycle when it's the only thing you are competing on and it creates and enforces a bad customer buying habit. Remember that when you lower prices, it's very difficult to go up again. So strategize on whether to use the price spice or simply serve up a generously portioned entree to the hungry value shopper in order to move customers from discounts to devotion.

CHAPTER SUMMARY

- The Price trigger redirects attention in a powerful way.

- Pricing can create bad customer habits. Too many businesses overuse the Price trigger and create discount wars in which customers become loyal to your price, not you.

- Price discounting can be applied to digital habit formation as a:
    - Spice – Sparingly on top of programs primarily driven by other triggers such as Peers & Power.
    - Entree – The attraction as the low-cost provider in the Value Quadrant of the Timeographic Framework, such as Wal-mart.

- Build loyalty to you and not your price through value-added features.

- Developing a niche and using price discounting sparingly to close the deal is another way to differentiate in price-competitive markets. Design is key.

TAKE-AWAY QUESTIONS

- Do you dish up price as a spice or as an entree in your marketing campaigns? What percentage of the time is it applied relative to the other triggers?

- If you apply it as an entree, is your organization set up to be the low-cost provider?

- If not, what tools and methods can you leverage that foster building a relationship with customers to move them from discounts to devotion?

- How can you combine the price trigger with one or more of the other triggers as a spice to build a habit?

CONCLUSION

Accelerating the Customer Journey

•))

From Distraction to Traction

Although it was Hillary Rodham Clinton who ushered the phrase 'it takes a village' into popular usage with her book, *It Takes a Village: And Other Lessons Children Teach Us*, it was Pampers and P&G who could be credited with using the same concept for their wildly successful social community, the Pampers Village website and mobile app.

The Pampers Village digital strategy wonderfully illustrates how to bring all five customer triggers together to create digital habits and achieve traction through the mastery of time and attention innovation. Let's go step by step through the five triggers to analyze how they are applied in the Pampers Village concept.

Peers & Power

Users engage with peers in this vibrant online community, which has pregnancy and parenthood in common. Gamification (remember, it's a digital habit ecosystem and an ultimate Time Magnet) is utilized for tracking pregnancy progress. Grow On is another gamified feature that offers "amazing gifts" throughout the year for entering one code from a box of diapers or wipes each month onto the P&G website.[1]

Remember that friends and influencers trigger six times more traffic and two times more conversions when they share content on social networks.[2] That's a lot of power. In Pampers Village, the homepage, product pages, and order confirmation page all have social sharing buttons. The related Hello Baby app allows busy moms to be mobile with these tools,[3] enabling them to share items of common interest with friends from their Lamaze or Mommy & Me classes – a classic example of inserting P&G offers into a customer routine that promotes rapid adoption and repeat purchases.

Personal Pursuits

Pampers Village is a fun and festive online destination. As you'll recall from Chapter 2, Personal Pursuit Triggers, often involves learning. With the 'Pampers Village Pregnancy Tracker', users can read and learn the exciting details of what is going on with each stage of their baby's development. Customized newsletters are sent out weekly to attract users to the site. 'Dads Are Expecting Too' is a section where users can find articles written specifically for dads and allows P&G to cross-promote other products such as Fusion razors, because "everything that touches a baby's skin should be soft, including Dad's face."[4]

There's entertainment, in the form of original content and a documentary web series that is very high quality and complete with cliffhangers, such as ending a webisode with expectant parents about to learn the sex of their baby. Users can also watch more practical video content made by the Pampers Parenting Network – a group of experts and medical professionals who offer advice on things such as breastfeeding, car seat installation, nutrition, potty training, and more.[5]

Another vital element of Pampers Village that taps into the Personal Pursuits trigger is the charitable campaigns, such as Little Miracle Mission, which donates care packages to families with babies in neonatal intensive care units. This creates lots of feel-good emotions, leaving members of the community feeling very positive about both themselves and the brand.

Prairie Dog Event

Pregnancy is a life stage event that is one of the most exciting and joyous times of many peoples' lives. Everyone wants the best for their baby and there's so much to do that you never had to think about before. To say that it's a time when lots of new habits are being formed would be an understatement. You'll recall from Chapter 3 that Prairie Dog Events occupy the Habit quadrant. A Prairie Dog event involves a change being made. New habits will be formed to reflect that change.

A first baby is one of the few Prairie Dog triggers in life when expectant parents will not worry about budgets to buy new items. Not knowing what the real deal entails, they will happily buy the latest gadget or gizmo for junior because well-heeled parents want "the best."

Remember that habit development doesn't stop with the customer placing the order. It must continue until the customer is fully functional and has adopted your product. What makes all the difference here is a personal level of engagement that extends across social media, service lines, in-store, and mobile. When Pampers came under fire for their Dry Max line of diapers that was thought to be causing severe diaper rash in babies, influential mommy bloggers were flown to headquarters to give their feedback and discuss the problem. The influential bloggers met with executives and scientists who addressed their questions. This approach was a big PR win, as the Pampers Village community saw it as meaningful engagement. P&G was not about to let a product snafu turn into a negative Prairie Dog event that caused their customers to go elsewhere. P&G contends that their efforts to address the concerns from a small but vocal set of customers resulted a year later in generating the largest market share for Pampers in the US in 10 years.[6]

Productivity

It's a brilliant achievement for Pampers Village to be able to keep users on their site for long periods of time, while simultaneously giving them the satisfaction of feeling productive. In this instance, productivity is triggered by being able to do so much on one website.

They can shop, of course, and the more they learn about through the content, the more they realize they need to buy. All moms have their lists, and this one-stop shopping experience allows them to tick through to-do items faster while also squeezing in reading a useful article or donating their points to benefit a worthy organization.

And just to show that Pampers Village creators have thought of everything, users can even plan a baby shower on the site. There are plans, checklists, and creative ideas to help get yet another thing done. Planning, purchasing, learning parenting – all of these things deliver incredible value in exchange for the time spent on the site.

> *Digital Habit Tip*: Brain habits require repetition to form a habit, yet repetition can break a Digital Habit.
>
> *Bottom Line*: Mix it up and make music! Customers want to hear delightful melodies, not the same monotone note, when engaging with their favorite brands.

Price

Pampers Village offers a robust rewards program. As mentioned above under Peers & Power, some aspects of this have been gamified in thematically appropriate ways. Entering codes from purchased products can be used to enter sweepstakes, donate to foundations, or to earn products. Purchases can be converted into points for toys, baby must-haves, and coupons, and there are plenty of members-only deals. There's no question that Pampers spices it up with price, but clearly, they are winning hearts, minds, and habits – a much more important victory.

Digital Customer Engagement

Now that we have an example of all the triggers working together, we can see how they actually function much like a complete ecosystem. If the goal is to incent users to spend as much time as possible with your business that means each trigger and reward habit must be reinforced. Successful companies accomplish this through the use of the following tools:

- **Sounds** –Imagine the "ding" from a new text arriving.

- **Messaging and Guilty Reminders** – RSVP anyone?

- **Visuals** – An infographic can say it all. The brain processes visuals sixty thousand times faster than text, according to one theory.[7] This tool is particularly powerful with harried business executives.

- **Defaults** – People do not like to change because habits save time.

- **Behavior-Driven Incentives** – Providing offers based on digital user preferences and algorithms.

- **Mobile Tech** – The rise of sensors and always-on gadgets create a cornucopia of opportunities.

Triggers Lead to Habit:
Technology Reinforces Behavior Change

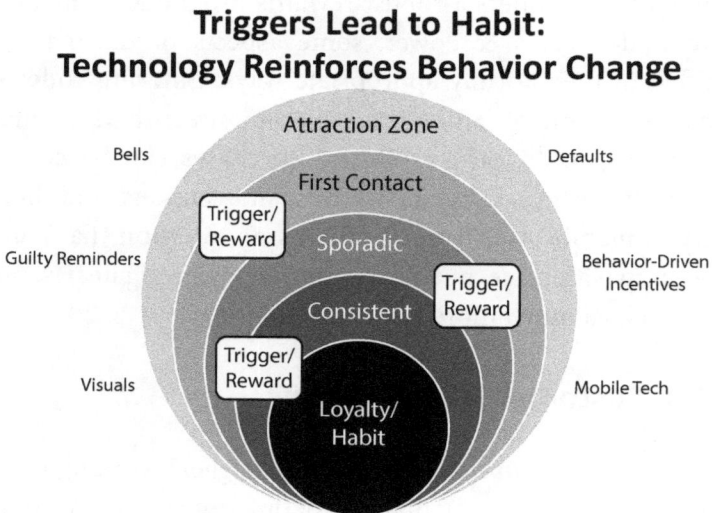

Figure C-1: From Distraction to Traction in the Customer Journey

As discussed in the Introduction, the concentric circles in Figure C-1 represent the way customers are nurtured by small triggers or ecosystem on-ramps, followed by a reward to convert into the next inner circle of adoption. Each of these trigger and reward habits are reinforced by the aforementioned tactics.

Digital Habit Tip: Test alternative reward and trigger structures in your customer journey through A/B, multivariate, and eye-tracking technology to optimize and understand customer reactions. User experience (UX) designers or website experts are great resources.

Bottom Line: Little tests over time can lead to big results.

An additional element in the outer ring of this system is the rise of what we call the Attraction Zone. Since anyone can and will research your firm online and poll peers about the performance of your offering, your Attraction Zone becomes an additional element to manage in your marketing mix. The best ways to effectively identify and manage this are addressed in our book about managing the Business Reputation Zone in the Exponential Influence® book series.

Digital Habit Ecosystems

How will we ever reach our destination if we don't see where we're headed? That's why maps are so useful. A case in point is how Pampers Village uses mobile updates and electronic widgets. Each week, the expectant parent receives an update on their baby's development. This allows P&G to track due dates and engage customers as their baby grows – and to provide perfectly timed parenting advice and product offerings that fit each stage.

Another example of continued efforts toward a complete ecosystem is with the latest Apple software system, Yosemite. (Some users already miss the big cats, but Apple has roared that it's time to move on.) In her article "Apple Wants All of You," Lily Hay Newman writes, "Numerous features Apple announced are aimed squarely at Google": The update includes new features in Spotlight, the search tool on an Apple computer.[8]

As before, Spotlight searches your local content. But now, if you search the name of a movie, for example, you'll be shown show times at your local theaters as well as related content available on iTunes. Spotlight is also now integrated with the Safari browser so that when you enter a URL, you will be given "Spotlight suggestions." Newman writes that, "These Spotlight features are largely contingent on your participation in the total Apple ecosystem."[9] To begin with, you need a Mac to run Yosemite. You also need to use Mail for email and iCal for your calendar in order for local data to come up in a Spotlight search. But to be fully integrated, you need to use Safari as your browser. As the headline says, *Apple wants all of you*. They want to capture and claim you as their own so that you're not tempted to ever buy a Google product.

> *Digital Habit Tip*: Guide your customers to key action - never force or lock in customers or flight instincts will take hold. How would Louis XIV handle this?
>
> *Bottom Line*: Apply digital habits ethically - influence and nurture, but do not force.

What's happening here is that neither company is happy about the market fragmentation that comes with consumers using combinations like Google Drive and iPhoto. Their answer to this is to create features that will force users to commit to their entire ecosystem.[10] Such habits create a strong competitive advantage with rich data about customer behaviors and preferences that will drive profitability.

Your Action Plan

How can you get started? The simplified diagram in describes a process we have used with clients in which we map triggers and rewards onto the customer journey:

First, customer journey maps should be developed with key customer segments, geographies, and preferences in mind. Identify key interactions and map out the key habit triggers and rewards throughout the customer's experience.

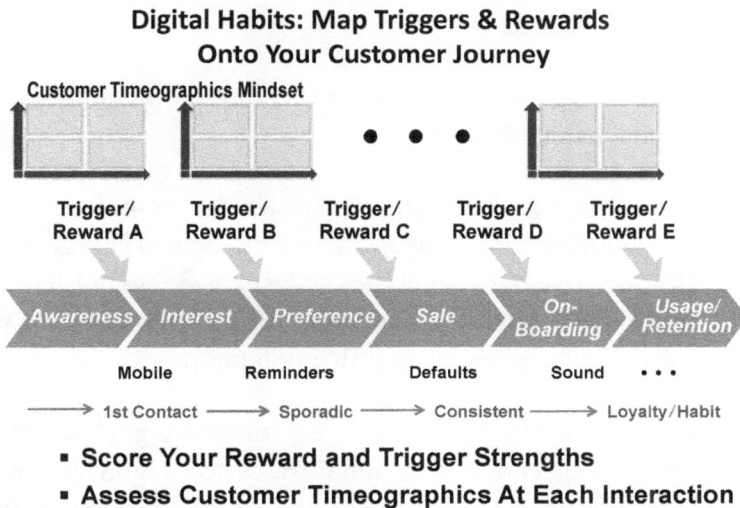

Digital Habits: Map Triggers & Rewards Onto Your Customer Journey

Customer Timeographics Mindset

Trigger/ Reward A   Trigger/ Reward B   Trigger/ Reward C   Trigger/ Reward D   Trigger/ Reward E

Awareness › Interest › Preference › Sale › On-Boarding › Usage/Retention

Mobile   Reminders   Defaults   Sound   • • •

1st Contact ——→ Sporadic ——→ Consistent ——→ Loyalty/Habit

- **Score Your Reward and Trigger Strengths**
- **Assess Customer Timeographics At Each Interaction**

Figure C-2 Applying and Assessing Digital Habits, Triggers and Timeographics In Your Customer Journey

Second, ensure that the digital habit on-ramps that you have defined are in line with customer time and attention constraints and preferences. At each stage of the journey, you should assess the Timeographics mindset of the customer at each interaction i.e. what time of the day and week is it? Is there a potential Prairie Dog event? Will the customer likely triage the interaction as something she would likely to devote time? Or will it be in the middle of a rushed workday for an executive who would be likely to have a time savings or time minimized mindset?

Third, score and assess these interactions to identify the areas of your customer journey that are strong and weak in terms of customer engagement. This process enables us to answer the following questions:

- Where do we find the most leakage in the customer experience?

- What is the customer's Timeographic mindset at each point of interaction?

- List the trigger(s) involved at each key customer interaction (digital habit on-ramp).

- Are the triggers creating the digital habit on-ramp aligned with the customer Timeographics at that moment of engagement? How does each trigger at each stage map to Figure I-5 in the Introduction? Could other triggers be better suited given the customer Timeographics at that point in time?

- Are you over-relying on one type of method, digital reinforcement or trigger that could annoy the customer and ultimately break the digital habit? I recall a cloud software company that like a bad dream continuously sent the same email day after day from their system.

- How strong are the rewards relating to the trigger? Can we reinforce them with technology to build a digital habit?

- How frictionless are your interactions? Do you make it as simple as possible for customers to progress and interact with you more?

To better understand how time and attention constraints affect customer decision-making and Timeographics, refer to my book, *The 24-Hour Customer*. Lastly, check out our websites at exponentialinfluence.com and exponentialedge.com for additional tips, worksheets, and articles.

I hope you have found helpful ideas and methods from this book that you can rapidly apply to your business to establish profitable digital habit techniques or to develop complete digital habit ecosystems.

It is easier to identify the pitfalls that strike many digital marketers today because we now know that digital habits are different than traditional habits. Through such techniques, you can leverage the powerful synergy of technology with human neuroscience and motivation in order to prompt behavior change and form digital habits that rapidly grow your brand in today's distraction-filled economy.

ABOUT THE AUTHOR

Adrian C. Ott
Award-Winning Author, CEO, and Speaker

*"One of Silicon Valley's most respected
(if not the most respected) strategists."*
Consulting Magazine

Adrian C. Ott is CEO and Founder of Exponential Edge Inc. consulting, which is headquartered in Silicon Valley. She and her team have produced tangible results in the areas of market strategy, routes-to-market and new product concepts for companies such as: Microsoft, P&G, Ricoh, EMC, and venture-funded start-ups. In 2014, she was honored as one of the most inspiring women leaders in Northern California by the Harvard Business School.

Adrian is also the award-winning author of *The 24-Hour Customer: New Rules for Winning in a Time-Starved, Always-Connected Economy* (HarperBusiness) which was named Best Business Book of the Year by Library Journal, USA Book News and Small Business Trends magazines.

Adrian is an expert contributor to Fast Company and her work has been featured in Harvard Business Review, Strategy & Leadership Journal, and other major publications. She has been interviewed on Bloomberg TV, Fox News, The Washington Post and Forbes.

In addition to keynotes for corporate meetings and industry events, Adrian regularly lectures at major business schools such as USC, Carnegie Mellon, Stanford, and the University of California.

Prior to founding Exponential Edge, she was an HP executive for 15 years, and led the HP Garage Program for start-ups. She was recognized for her work in an annual report for "infusing HP with new revenue streams, new technologies, and new business models." She holds an MBA from Harvard Business School and a B.S. from U.C. Berkeley.

Awards and Honors

50 Marketing Thought Leaders List, 2014, Brand Quarterly magazine

Harvard Business School Most Inspiring Women Leaders in Northern California, 2014

Silicon Valley Enterprising Woman of the Year Award, 2011, NAWBO-SV (one honoree per year)

50 Marketing Leaders to Know List. Global CMO Magazine, 2013

The Best Business Book of the Year Award, 2011, USA Book News

Best Business Book of the Year Award, 2010 Library Journal

Best Business Book of the Year Award, 2010 Small Business Trends

#1 on Stanford Business School Summer Recommended Reading List, 2012

#1 Business Bestseller, Shanghai Daily (China)

Editors' Commended Paper Award, 2012, Strategy & Leadership Journal

Recognized in an HP Annual Report for "Infusing HP with new revenue streams, new technologies and new business models."

Connect With Adrian:

LinkedIn: www.linkedin.com/in/adrianott/
ExponentialEdge.com
ExponentialInfluence.com
Twitter: @ExponentialEdge

INDEX

A

Aaker, David ii
Abraham, Stanley Iv
Abrams, Rhonda 74
Airbnb 61
Airhelp 62
Alexa 40
Amazon 6, 13, 14, 53
Amazon Prime 53
American Association Of Family Physicians 64
Americana, The 38
AOL 50
Apple 13, 37, 41, 86
Aristotle 47
Arnesen, Erna v
AT&T 52
Attention Span, Goldfish 5

B

Behavior Triggers 19
Best Buy 69
Bing 11
Blasingame, Jim ii
Bocska, Steve 33
Brand Vines 5
Brigham Young University 14

C

Cal Poly Pomona iv
Can I Park Here 60
Carlsbad, California 39
Caruso, Rick 38
Chaffin, Janice iii
Chamberlain, Sheryl v
Chow, Jim v
Clifford, Stephanie 70
CMS Wire 50
Coca-Cola 29
Coldplay 42
Comcast 19
Computer Routines 11, 12, 20, 22, 23
Consulting Magazine . . . . ii, 90

D

Daily Deal. 33
Datagravity 73, 74
Digital Habit Formation. 6
Digital Habit Formation, Triggers and. 6
Digital Habit Tip . . .   2, 4, 6, 9, 28, 33, 42, 43, 52, 53, 55, 61, 63, 70, 72, 83, 85, 86
Disney. 1, 2, 3, 4, 3
Disney Experience, My 1
Disrupt NY 2014 63
Draper, Don 17
Dryel. 8

E

Engen, Jerry. 39
Exponential Edge. . . . . iv, vi, viii
Exponential Influence . . . . vi, 6, 19

F

Facebook 62
Farmville 32
5Ps, The 20
Fixed. 62
Fix In Six 5
Fomo (Fear Of Missing Out) 14, 15
Forbes 90
Foursquare 43
Franklin, Benjamin 59

G

Game Of Thrones 28
Gamification 80
Ghost Stories 42
Gmail 19
Google. 11, 12
GPS 12
Groupon. 33
Grove, The 38
Guilty Reminders 26, 27, 28, 35, 36, 84
Guitar Center. 41

H

Habit Formation 6, 7
Habit-Goal Interface. 8
Habits, Brain 11
Habits, Digital 2, 6, 11, 13, 15
Hao, Ping iii
Happiness Arcade 29
Harvard Business School Association iii
Hastings, Reed 47
Hayzlett, Jeffrey. ii
Hungerford, Amede iv

I

IBM 50
Iger, Robert 4
Inc.com 74
Industry Building Blocks Iv
Ingram, Katie. 50
Instagram 62
Instagram Diet 14
iPhone. 26
iTunes 86

J

Jetsons. 13
Jones, Casey. 60

K

Kayak 18
Killerstartups.com 65
Kuo, Ivan 33

L

Lincoln, Abraham 37
Lohr, Steve 50
Long, Paula. 73
Louis XIV. 26
Lowe's 5

M

Mad Men 17
Marriott. 32
Martin, Chris 42
Medicast. 65
Mehta, Sanjay. Iv

Michaels, Alan S.. iv
Michaelsen, Nicolas 63
Microsoft 11
Monkey Parking 61
Mozilla 50
Mymagic+. 1, 2, 3

N

NBA 43
Netflix. 47, 48, 49
Netsuite Iv
Newman, Lily Hay 86
New York Times 50, 70
Nielson 40
NPR Marketplace 38

O

Ogilvy Public Relations 5

P

Pampers. 79, 80, 81, 82, 83, 85
Parking Panda 18
Parkme 60
Parkopedia 60
Peers & Power . . . . , 76, 20, 71
Perry, Katy 4
Personal Pursuits. 20
Personal Pursuits Trigger 73
P&G 8, 9
Phocus Wright 2
Pink Nation. 42
Pinterest. 34
Polk Automotive 53
Power Triggers 27, 34
Power Triggers 25, 27, 35
Poythress, Katherine. 39
Prairie Dog Events . . . . , 56, 49, 57, 57, 20
Prairie Dog Triggers 49
Price 20
Prius, Toyota 53
Productivity. 20
Productivity Trigger 59, 62
Pug Pharm Productions. 33

Q

Quinby, Douglas 2

R

Rasulo, Jay. 3
Reputation Zone 85
Ricoh Innovations iv
Royal Albert Hall. 42
RSVP 84

S

San Diego Union Tribune, The 39
Schwietzer, Robbie. 54
Sims, The 32
Siri. 12
Southwest Airlines 73
Spotlight. 86
Staggs, Tom 3
Standard Parking. 60
Statisticbrain.com 5
Symantec iii

T

Take Care Clinics. 64
Tapas And Tasting Menus. 4, 5
Taylor, Heather 5
Tesla 53
Time Magnets 16, 17
Time Minimizers. 16
Timeographics 16, 17, 19, 20, 21, 22, 23
Time On Autopilot. 16, 19
Time Savers 16, 18
T-Mobile 52
Toyota 53
Triggers And Digital Habit Formation. 6
Triggers, Technology, And Habits 6, 16
24-Hour Customer, The 51
Twitter. 5

U

Uber 61, 65
Ullrich, Kathryn iii
U.C. Berkeley ii

V

Variety 4
Versailles 26
Victoria's Secret 42
Vine 5
Voicepark 60
Volvo 60

W

Walgreens 64
Wal-Mart 69, 76
Wells Fargo 55
Westfield Group 39
Whatsapp 43
Williams-Sonoma 40
Wired Magazine 53

Z

Zappos 32

NOTES

Introduction: Triggers, Technology, and Habits

1 Christopher Palmeri, "Disney Bets $1 Billion on Technology to Track Theme-Park Visitors," Business Week, March 7, 2014, http://www.businessweek.com/articles/2014-03-07/disney-bets-1-billion-on-technology-to-track-theme-park-visitors

2 Ibid

3 Ibid

4 Ibid

5 Ibid

6 Bob Lefsetz, "Katy Perry's 'Prism' a Good Example of How Albums Don't Work Anymore." Variety, November 13, 2013; U.S. Edition, Accessed on 7/1/2014 via http://variety.com/2013/biz/news/katy-perrys-prism-a-good-example-of-how-albums-dont-work-anymore-1200824933/

7 Edward Helmore, "Is the Album Dead? Katy Perry, Miley Cyrus and Elton John hit by dramatic US Sales Slump." The Guardian, November 2, 2013, Accessed 7/1/14 at http://www.theguardian.com/music/2013/nov/02/is-music-album-dead-us-worst-ever-sales-figures

8 Tara Urso, "Instagram, Vine and Marketing to Our Short Attention Spans," Social Media Today, August 22, 2013, http://socialmediatoday.com/tara-urso/1683551/instagram-vine-marketing-our-short-attention-spans.

9 To view an example of Lowes YouTube video: http://j.mp/1nCKCWv

10 Harald Weinreich, Hartmut Obendorf, Eelco Herder, and Matthias Mayer, "Not Quite The Average: An Empirical Study Of Web Use," ACM Transactions on the Web, 2, no. 1 (February 2008), Article No. 5, DOI.

11 Tom, "Fat Habits," Duke Research Blog, Duke University, February 28, 2008, http://dukeresearch.blogspot.com/2008_02_03_archive.html.

12 Mindy Ji Song and Wendy Wood,"Habitual Purchase and Consumption Habits: Not Always What You Intend," Journal of Consumer Psychology 17(4), 2007: 261-276.

13 Dryel was sold by P&G to another firm in 2008.

14 Comscore market share analysis, February 2014 and prior years.

15 Larson et all, "How Instagram Can Ruin Your Dinner," , October 3, 2013, Brigham Young University Press Release accessed October 1 20114 at http://news.byu.edu/archive13-oct-instagramfood.aspx Study originally published in Journal of Consumer Psychology.

NOTES

Chapter 1: Peers & Power Triggers

1   Adrian Ott, "Time Magnets: Louis XIV, Social Strategy, and Games," Fast Company, March 25, 2011, http://www.fastcompany.com/1742616/time-magnets-louis-xiv-social-strategy-and-games.

2   Sumit Dutta, "40 Must-See Charts for Modern Marketers," slide 12, Oracle Eloqua Lead Generation Slideshare, August 15 2013, http://www.slideshare.net/SKDream/40-must-see-charts-for-modern-marketers.

3   George R.R. Martin, "A Game of Thrones: A Song of Ice and Fire Book One," Game of Thrones, HBO TV Series, 2013 – present, http://www.georgerrmartin.com/grrm_book/a-game-of-thrones-a-song-of-ice-and-fire-book-one/ and http://www.hbo.com/game-of-thrones#/.

4   Jeff Beer, "To Encourage Recycling, Coke Made A Game Powered By Empty Plastic Bottles," Fast to Create, April 28, 2014, http://www.fastcocreate.com/3029801/to-encourage-recycling-coke-made-an-arcade-game-powered-by-empty-plastic-bottles.

5   To view a YouTube video of the Coke Happiness Arcade, https://www.youtube.com/watch?v=MFXOs0lHRys

6   Adam Kleinberg, "Brands that failed with gamification," iMedia Connection, July 23, 2012, http://www.imediaconnection.com/content/32284.asp#singleview.

7   Ibid.

8   Ibid.

9   Ivan Kuo, "Gamification Pitfalls: Badge Fatigue and Loyalty Backlash," Gamification, September 12, 2012, http://www.gamification.co/2012/09/12/gamification-pitfalls-badge-fatigue-and-loyalty-backlash/

10 Ibid.

11 Ibid.

12 Urfan Ahmad, "30+ Statistics How Social Media Influence Purchasing Decisions [INFOGRAPHIC}," Socialmedia Today, January 24, 2014, http://socialmediatoday.com/irfan-ahmad/2108426/30-statistics-how-social-media-influence-purchasing-decisions-infographic.

Chapter 2: Personal Pursuit Triggers

1 According to www.carusoaffiliated.com "Sales per square feet at Caruso centers are 75% higher than industry averages. 93% of all guests make a purchase and the average expenditure at a Caruso center is nearly double the norm for an enclosed regional mall." Accessed 7/3/2014 at http://carusoaffiliated.com/caruso/the_company/overview.php

2 Todd Longwell, "Mall Builder Rick Caruso Expands to Pacific Palisades," Variety, February 26, 2014, http://variety.com/2014/biz/features/mall-builder-rick-caruso-expands-to-pacific-palisades-1201121983/ .

3 Kai Ryssdal, "Malls are dead, long live the mall," NPR Marketplace Corner Office, April 17, 2014, http://www.marketplace.org/topics/business/corner-office/malls-are-dead-long-live-mall

4 Katherine Poythress, "Carlsbad mall reaches for 'beach chic,'" U~T San Diego, April 28, 2014, http://www.utsandiego.com/news/2014/Apr/28/westfield-carlsbad-renovation/ .

5 Ibid.

6 Ibid.

7 Editor's Pick, "Coldplay Hides New Album's Lyrics in Libraries Around the World," http://www. Creativity-Online.com, May 1, 2014. Accessed on 7/3/2014 at http://creativity-online.com/work/coldplay-ghost-stories-scavenger-hunt/35206

8 Darrell Etherington, "Facebook Acquires Fitness And Activity Tracking App Moves," TechCrunch, April 24, 2014, http://techcrunch.com/2014/04/24/facebook-acquires-activity-tracking-app-moves/ .

Chapter 3: Prairie Dog Events

1   Greg Sandoval, "Netflix's Lost Year: The Inside Story of the Price-Hike Train Wreck," CNET, July 11, 2012, http://www.cnet.com/news/netflixs-lost-year-the-inside-story-of-the-price-hike-train-wreck/

2   Ibid.

3   Jason Gilbert, "Netflix Price Hike's One Year Anniversary: A Look Back At One Of The Great Tech Blunders," Huffington Post, July 12, 2012, http://www.huffingtonpost.com/2012/07/12/netflix-price-hike-anniversary_n_1668382.html .

4   Jocelyn Richard, "23 Ridiculous Netflix FAILS (PICTURES)," Huffington Post, November 11, 2011, http://www.huffingtonpost.com/2011/09/21/23-netflix-fails-pictures_n_973461.html

5   Adam Hartung, "Netflix – The Turnaround Story of 2012!"Forbes, January 29, 2013, http://www.forbes.com/sites/adamhartung/2013/01/29/netflix-the-turnaround-story-of-2012/.

6   Katie Ingram, "IBM: US$83 Billion Lost Yearly in Marketing Due to Poor Customer Experience,"CMS Wire, May 29, 2013, http://www.cmswire.com/cms/customer-experience/ibm-us83-billion-lost-yearly-in-marketing-due-to-poor-customer-experience-021084.php .

7   Steve Lohr, "The Default Choice, So Hard to Resist," The New York Times, October 15, 2011, http://www.nytimes.com/2011/10/16/technology/default-choices-are-hard-to-resist-online-or-not.html?_r=0 .

8   Damon Lavrinc, "Tesla Keeps Poaching Prius Buyers, and It's Not Slowing Down," Wired, March 17, 2014, http://www.wired.com/2014/03/tesla-model-s-toyota-prius/ .

9   Brad Tuttle, "Amazon Prime: Bigger, more Powerful, More Profitable than Anyone Imagined," Time, March 18, 2013, http://business.time.com/2013/03/18/amazon-prime-bigger-more-powerful-more-profitable-than-anyone-imagined/.

10 Ibid.

11 Ibid.

12 Ibid.

13 Alexis Kleinman, "Amazon Hiking Price of Prime to $99," Huffingon Post, March 13, 2014, http://www.huffingtonpost.com/2014/03/13/amazon-prime-price_n_4955631.html .

Chapter 4: Productivity Triggers

1 This claim is according to VoicePark' s description of their service accessed on 7/5/2014 http://www.voicepark.org/about

2 Parkopedia Press Release, "Parkopedia to Power Volvo Car Groups Global in-car Parking Service," PRNewswire, November 19, 2013, http://www.prnewswire.com/news-releases/parkopedia-to-power-volvo-car-groups-global-in-car-parking-service-232500661.html.

3 Jaclyn Trop, "Secret Weapon in Mall Battle: Parking Apps," The New York Times, November 27, 2013, http://www.nytimes.com/2013/11/28/business/secret-weapon-in-mall-battle-parking-apps.html?pagewanted=all&_r=0.

4 Terri Collins, "San Francisco Warns Monkey To Stop Selling Spots," ABC News, June 23, 2014, http://abcnews.go.com/Technology/wireStory/san-francisco-warns-monkey-stop-selling-spots-24265389.

5 According to the Fixed description of services accessed 7/5/2014 at http://www.getfixed.me

6 Romain Dillet, "Airhelp Lets You Claim Money For Messed Up Flights," TechCrunch, May 6, 2014, http://techcrunch.com/2014/05/06/with-airhelp-claim-money-for-messed-up-flights/.

7 Ibid.

8 Ibid.

9 Ibid

10 Keith Liles, "Feeling Ill? Don't Move. Have Medicast Bring the Doctor to You," KillerStartups, April 1, 2013, http://www.killerstartups.com/startup-spotlight/medicast-house-call-doctors-on-demand/

Chapter 5: Price Triggers

1 Stephanie Clifford, "Retail Frenzy: Prices on the Web Change Hourly," The New York Times, November 30, 2012, http://www.nytimes.com/2012/12/01/business/online-retailers-rush-to-adjust-prices-in-real-time.html?pagewanted=all&_r=0.

2 Corporate Fact Sheet, Southwest Airlines, accessed June 25, 2014, http://www.swamedia.com/channels/Corporate-Fact-Sheet/pages/corporate-fact-sheet.

3 Geri Stengel, "How To Carve Out A Niche And Raise $42 million in Venture Capital," Forbes, June 19, 2013, http://www.forbes.com/fdc/welcome_mjx.shtml.

4 Rhonda Abrams, "Competing on Price Alone," Inc., August 27,2002, http://www.inc.com/articles/2002/08/24551.html.

Conclusion: Accelerating the Customer Journey

1   Pampers website https://en.giftstogrow.pampers.com/index.html accessed 7/8/2014

2   Heather Taylor, "How Brands Can Win on Instagram and Vine," The Drum, July 12, 2013, http://www.thedrum.com/opinion/2013/07/12/how-brands-can-win-instagram-and-vine.

3   Pampers Apps and More page, Pampers, June 25, 2014, http://www.pampers.com/apps-and-more/newborn.

4   Ibid.

5   News flash, "P&G expands Pampers Village," Cincinnati Business Courier, November 13, 2008.

6   Jack Neff, "After Big Stink Over Dry Max, P&G Says Its Sales Are Stronger," AdAge, Sept. 2, 2001, http://adage.com/article/news/big-stink-dry-max-p-g-sales-stronger/229620/.

7   Timothy Gangwer, Visual Teaching, Corwin Press, 2009 pp. 37 "3M Corporation found the brain processes visuals sixty thousand time faster than it processes text..." (3MCorporation, 2001) accessed 7/8/20014 http://books.google.com/books?id=WZNyAwAAQBAJ&pg=PA37&dq=%223M+corporation+found+the+brain+processes+visuals+sixty+thousand+times+faster%22&hl=en&sa=X&ei=os-8U9HVBc_roASW7YGoAQ&ved=0CB4Q6AEwAA#v=onepage&q=%223

8   Lily Hay Newman, "Apple Wants All of You," Slate, June 2, 2014, http://www.slate.com/articles/technology/technology/2014/06/apple_wwdc_2014_apple_takes_aim_at_google.html.

9   Ibid.

10 Ibid.

The 24-Hour Customer

New Rules for Winning in a Time-Starved, Always-Connected Economy (Harper Collins)

by Adrian C. Ott

24HourCustomer.com

The Best Business Book of the Year
2011, USA Book News

Best Business Book of the Year
2010, Library Journal

Recommended Summer Reading List
Stanford Graduate School of Business
2012

#1 Business Bestseller
Shanghai Daily News, Amazon

**Best Business Book of the Year
Editor's Choice Award**
2010, Small Business Trends

**Best Business Book of the Year
Reader's Choice Award**
2010, Small Business Trends

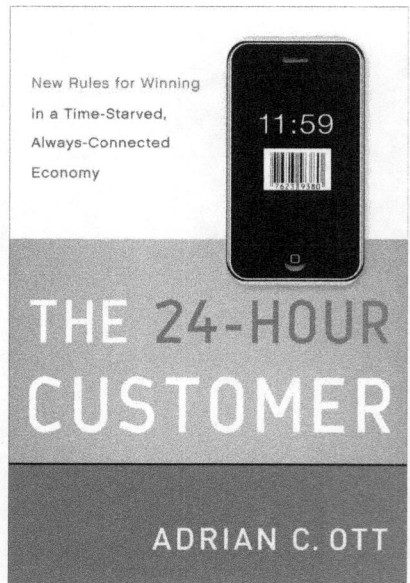

"Ott is revolutionizing marketing by adding the concept of time."

- Library Journal

www.ingramcontent.com/pod-product-compliance
Lightning Source LLC
Chambersburg PA
CBHW031947190326
41519CB00007B/698